Wheat Grass: From The Soil to Your Soul

A Complete Guide to Wheat Grass

By

Billye Graham

ISBN: 1-4107-0593-5 (e-book)
ISBN: 1-4107-0594-3 (Paperback)

Library of Congress Control Number: 2002096734

This book is printed on acid free paper.

Printed in the United States of America
Bloomington, IN

1st Books - rev. 01/15/04

Notice to Readers:

The health procedures outlined in this book are based on the training, research and personal experiences of the author. Natural healing often produces a healing crisis and given our individuality there is always the risk of adverse detoxification effects. Please do not use this book if you are unwilling to assume the risk.

ACKNOWLEDGEMENTS

I am good at details, organization and making things easy to understand. This work goes far beyond my talents. It is truly a group effort and I have many people to thank for it's content, continuity and completion.

Hiawatha Cromer – I thank you for constantly opening up new worlds and vistas of information to me.

David A. Graham III – I thank you son for loving me unconditionally and supporting me in all things.

Mrs. JohnnieRenee Nelson – I thank you for constantly encouraging me to get my "literary career" rolling.

Mr. Allen Davis – I thank you for being there for me, time and time again.

Sister Sarah Wallace – I thank you for reminding me of my path and to do God's work.

Thelma Curtis and Ada Cooper-Robinson – I thank you for teaching me all you knew about wheat grass.

Dr. Ruth Hamilton and Dr. Alfred Opubor - I thank you for mentoring and putting me in touch with "the teacher" in me.

All My Clients - I thank you for the satisfaction I have gotten from being of service to you. You are my "greatest teachers."

Dedication

"I DEDICATE THIS TREATISE ON WHEAT GRASS
TO HIAWATHA CROMER. THROUGH HER
KNOWLEDGE AND ASSISTANCE I HEALED MY
HEALTH CHALLENGE AND GREW WISE IN THE
WAYS OF THE UNIVERSE."

TABLE OF CONTENTS

INTRODUCTION

EXPERIENCE IS THE BEST TEACHER

MY TESTIMONIAL

My name is BILLYE GRAHAM and my personal crusade is health. I am not a doctor. I am a teacher. My gift is sharing information. What I would like to share with you is first hand knowledge about the healing powers of wheat grass. Faced with a serious HEALTH CHALLENGE, I ruled out surgery and embraced WHEAT GRASS THERAPY. The results were nothing less than amazing!

I went for a routine pap smear, during the summer of 1993, and experienced searing pain on the left side of my body. At the suggestion of my doctor an Ultra Sound Test was performed. The results were not due back for a week and I had a vacation planned. Upon my return I found several calls on my answering machine from my doctor and received calls from work and family saying to contact her office as soon as possible.

The Ultra Sound Test showed that my right ovary had developed a cyst measuring 6 by 4 centimeters and was enclosed in a sac of fluid and a mass had begun to form. At the time I was 44 years old. It is not abnormal for women in this age group to develop cysts and/or tumors. Often times they will shrink on their own. The concern, however, was over the mass that was forming, which suggested OVARIAN CANCER.

I listened intently while my doctor outlined her course of action, which was immediate exploratory surgery and signing off on a possible hysterectomy. I thanked her politely for her concern but informed her that the first thing I was going to do was put my hair in dreadlocks, and buy a van! If I was about to meet my maker I certainly wanted to look like who I really am.

Dreams deferred are often the root cause of disease. I felt a profound sense of shame. I had not taken good care of my spirit, or the body that houses it. I had forsaken myself to fulfill other's needs and desires. The end result was that I had compromised my health and strength in the process.

Armed with this realization, I began my personal crusade to recapture my treasures. I first sought a SECOND OPINION from a holistic practitioner, by the name of Jewel Prookrum. 8 hours later, carrying a list of products costing $500.00 and a hug for luck, I was told by Jewel "This cyst is active and it will either shrink or continue to grow. The choice is yours."

I knew instinctively that it was imperative that I take care of me with as few outside distractions as possible. I put my job on notice that I would be off indefinitely and I sent my son to stay with his father for the summer. After investigating several institutions that specialize in wheat grass therapy I decided upon a week long program at the SCHOOL

OF NATURAL HEALING, which is run by ADA COOPER, and located in Marshal, Michigan.

For those of you who have doubts and are reluctant to try wheat grass because you are experiencing a very serious health challenge, I just want to let you know that I too had doubts. I was about 95% sold on wheat grass, which was first introduced to me by Hiawatha Cromer, a family friend who runs the Creative Health Institute in Union city, Michigan. But, I had never faced a more serious health challenge so I arrived at Ada's with all my backup medicine and promptly informed her of my feelings. She assured me that I would not need them and she was right! The entire time I was there I never once felt the need to supplement my therapy with any of the herbs, teas or medicines that I had brought.

The first 3 days I went on a required FAST. On a daily basis I consumed 2 ounces of wheat grass in the morning and took three implants, morning, noon and night. The only other nourishment I consumed, for this 3-day period, was REJUVALAC (fermented wheat berries) and fresh carrot juice. The days were spent in classroom instruction, exercising and relaxation. As early as the second night I was more energized and felt far more confident that this was going to work for me.

On the 4th day I was introduced to living foods and how to prepare them. I learned to juice wheat grass and how to grow it. Both colon and massage therapy were made available, and I did both. By the end of the week I was walking up to 5 miles a day and sleeping only 4 to 6 hours a day. I was able to last twenty minutes doing rebounding exercises and lost 15 pounds in one week.

When I arrived at the School of Natural Healing my left foot just below the ankle had a dark overcast and the skin felt leathery to the touch. I had constant pain in this area. I understood from both my doctor and Ada, who does reflexology, that this area corresponds to the ovaries in the body. By the time I left the following week the spot was barely noticeable, the pain was almost gone and the skin was soft and supple again.

When I returned home I continued my wheat grass therapy and living foods regime. On August 23, 1993, precisely six weeks later, I re-took the Ultra Sound Exam. I was very confident that the test would not show anything abnormal. I felt great and even commented to the technician that she would not find anything. Everything was back to normal; the technician even brought in another colleague to re-check her diagnosis. They kept me there well over 20 minutes inquiring about wheat grass and how I had healed this health challenge in 28 days. My right ovary now measured 2 by 2 centimeters and there was no mass or fluid. I was not interested in knowing whether the cyst had been cancerous or not. I had healed and I had learned.

MRN: 1143862   NAME: GRAHAM, BILLYE
DATE: 07/08/93   ROOM: OPD

ORDER: PETER BARNOVSKY DO
       35000 SCHOOLCRAFT
       LIVONIA MI 48150

PELVIC ULTRASOUND STUDY WITH ABDOMINAL AND TRANSVAGINAL SCANNING
TECHNIQUES - PAIN - 07-08-93

PELVIC ULTRASOUND: The uterus is anteverted measuring 7.6 x 4.8 x 3.5
cm. No evidence of intrinsic abnormalities within the confines of the
uterus are identified. This study demonstrates the presence of a
septated cystic in the right ovary measures approximately 4 x 5 cm in
greatest diameter and probably represents a moderate size ovarian
cyst. The left ovary appears normal. No free fluid in the adnexal or
cul-de-sac areas were seen at this time.

IMPRESSION:

1.   Right ovarian cyst is identified. Pelvic ultrasound is otherwise
     normal.

                     SAMUEL JASSENOFF DO

/:   fcg   DT: 07/09/93
ACCT:0831453
ORDER#: 559923   559968
RADIOLOGY REPORT

BOTSFORD GENERAL (OSTEOPATHIC) - DEPARTMENT OF RADIOLOGY
27201   RADIOLOGIST

ST. MARY HOSPITAL
LIVONIA, MICHIGAN

RADIOLOGY REPORT

PATIENT:	GRAHAM, BILLYE J.	MR#:	484805	ACCT.#:	1813465
RADIOLOGIST:	Renuka Patel, M.D.			ROOM.#:	OPD
ATT. PHYS.:	DR. S. PARKS	DOB:	10/14/48	DATE OF EXAM:	8/23/93

8596 Canton Center Rd.
Canton, MI 48187

ULTRASOUND OF THE PELVIS

Multiple images were obtained using real time technique.

The approximate size of the uterus is 6.8 x 3.4 x 3.5 cm. The uterine
echogenicity appears unremarkable.

The approximate size of the right and left ovary is 2.0 x 1.1 x 2.0 cm. and 1.9
x 1.1 x 1.7 cm. No free fluid in the pelvis or abnormal pelvic mass.

IMPRESSION

The uterus and ovaries appear unremarkable. No abnormal pelvic mass or free
fluid in the pelvis.

BILATERAL LOW DOSE FILM SCREEN MAMMOGRAM

Each breast was examined in multiple projections. Comparison is made with the
previous outside films from Botsford Hospital dated 3-13-92.

No discrete spiculated malignant appearing mass, suspicious grouped
calcifications, nipple retraction, or skin thickening. No appreciable interval
change.

Previous Rt ovarian mass gone

XX

PATIENT: GRAHAM, BILLYE J.   MR#: 484805   ACCT.#: 1813465
RADIOLOGIST: Renuka Patel, M.D.   ROOM.#: OPD

PAGE 2

IMPRESSION

1. No mammographic evidence of malignancy. In the event of any palpable
    abnormality, its management should be based upon the clinical information.

2. I would recommend annual mammographic and continued physical examination
    for a patient of this age group.

Renuka Patel, M.D.

DD: 08/26/93
DT: 08/26/93
TR: ld

PART I:

FROM SOIL

Billye Graham

CHAPTER ONE

THE GRASS

IS

GREENER
ON THE
OTHER SIDE

Billye Graham

AN HISTORICAL OVERVIEW

The old adage that "the grass is greener on the other side," generally bespeaks of something better. When we look at grass in a different light and examine it carefully we indeed discover something extraordinary. It is more valuable than gold because no amount of money can buy you what it can give and restore – **GOOD HEALTH.**

The idea of obtaining health from grass is probably a foreign concept to most people. Grass is something we lay on when we're at a picnic; it is what we diligently cut in the summer time, what we play golf on and feed to horses, in the form of hay. However, we seem to be the only animals in the animal kingdom unaware, on an instinctive basis, of its medicinal properties.

If you are a pet owner, you are already familiar with what dogs and cats do when they get sick. **THEY EAT GRASS!** Nature has endowed them with the instinctual knowledge that grass is medicine. Animals that live on a high chlorophyll diet, such as the deer, hippopotamus, elephant, steer and horse each live strong, healthy and vital lives and are prone to only a few occasional diseases rather than the myriad that plague mankind.

The use of grass to fight dis-ease has not gone totally without human recognition; there is even a biblical reference. The Book of Daniel, 4th chapter verses 31 and 32, talks of King Nebuchadnezzar who lost his mental and physical well being. He was told by God to go out into the fields and "EAT GRASS AS DO THE OXEN." The king followed this advice and in time regained his sanity, his health and his throne.

Unless it is brought to our attention, few of us realize that grass is part of the CREATION STORY. In those first seven days, God was creating environmental essentials for the maintenance of life on earth. In the Book of Genesis, 1st chapter verse 11, God said "LET THE EARTH BRING FORTH GRASS." It is right up there with light and darkness, heaven and earth and the firmament. Grass was created before herbs, trees, animals or man. Along with water, air, and sunshine, grass is all we need to stay alive.

The knowledge of health from grass has been around for a long time. Both the Ancient Egyptians and the Chinese knew that grass was a powerful blood tonic. Scientific investigation that began back in the 1930's brought renewed interest in cereal grasses such as wheat grass. At the University of Wisconsin, Dr. George Kohler studied the difference in the nutrition value of cow's milk produced at different seasons of the year. He found that the highest nutritional value came from milk produced during the summer months when grazing cows consumed grass. (18)

In 1940, Drs. Kohler, Schnabel and Graham reported that cereal grasses contained a variety of high level and important vitamins, minerals and proteins. Years later, Dr. Hagiwara of Japan added enzymes as previously overlooked benefits of cereal grasses. And finally in 1979 Dr. Chiu-Nan Lai, of the University of Texas, presented evidence that wheat grass contains anti-cancer properties. (18)

It was the late Dr. Ann Wigmore who really popularized the use of wheat grass. She grew up against the backdrop of World War I and watched her grandmother in native Lithuania treat injured soldiers with grass poultices. She cured herself of gangrene while still in her teens and later in life again turned to wheat grass as her health failed due to the consumption of the Standard American Diet. (SAD). (21)

Dr. Ann discovered a revolutionary way of juicing wheat grass. Previously it was only available from pharmacies in a dehydrated form. Wheat grass juice led to popular demand by mainstream America. Soon people began to ask for it in juice bars, health spas and living foods centers across this land. She also taught people how to grow it for

pennies in the comfort of their own homes. Her "Living Foods Lifestyle" is now practiced at numerous health retreats throughout the world. (5)

CHAPTER TWO

"Let thy food be your medicine

And let your medicine be your food."

Hippocrates

(The Father of modern medicine)

Billye Graham

WHAT IS WHEAT GRASS?

There seems to be a lot of confusion about what wheat grass really is, even among those who use it regularly. I have heard many definitions ranging from "New Age Marijuana" to "plain old cow feed." **WHEAT GRASS IS ACTUALLY A VEGETABLE. IT IS CONSIDERED A CEREAL GRASS.** All grains such as wheat, rye, millet, barley and oats produce grasses before grains. Just before the stalk of grain begins to grow (the point of jointing) the grass is cut and harvested. An illustration of the jointing stage is shown on the next page.

Billye Graham

JOINTING

When wheat grass reaches its peak (six to eight inches) it begins to form a joint which will go on to produce the stalk of grain. Once jointing occurs, the nutritional level of the grass drops dramatically as the store nutrients are now needed for the production of the grain. Gluten is formed in the grain after wheat grass is harvested.

Joint

According to laboratory analysis done by Dr. Kohler, nutrients found in young green cereal plants vary with the <u>stage of growth</u> (from seed to plant to grain) rather than with the age or height of the plant. Chlorophyll, protein and most of the vitamins found in cereal grasses reach their peak concentrations in the period just prior to the jointing stage. This period only lasts for several days and represents the highest activity of photosynthesis and the culmination of the vegetation stage of the plant. After the jointing stage nutrients are concentrated in the cellulose stem that begins to grow. And in turn this powerhouse of nutrients is passed on to the stalk and eventually to the grain it produces (18).

Comparatively speaking, wheat grass contains about the same nutrients as other cereal grasses. Barley grass does seem to have a slightly higher nutritive concentration. My preference for wheat grass stems from its ready availability, its low cost and the ease with which it can be grown. When cereal grasses are compared to other vegetables however, they far surpass them in nutritive concentration. A comparison chart is shown on the next page.

Billye Graham

NUTRITIONAL COMPARISON
OF WHEAT GRASS
TO OTHER CEREAL GRASSES

VEGETABLE	WEIGHT gr.	PROTEIN gr.	FIBER gr.	CALCIUM mg.	VITAMIN A IU	IRON mg.	SELENIUM mcg.	MAGN mg.	POTASSIUM mg.
Dehydrated Wheat Grass	100	25.0	17.0	515	66,080	57.1	99.7	197.5	1,425
Beets (raw)	100	1.7	0.8	17	22	0.7	—	23.3	339
Bib Lettuce (raw)	100	1.3	0.5	35	964	2.1	—	9.0	264
Broccoli (raw)	100	3.6	1.5	103	2,500	1.1	—	24.0	382
Brussels Sprouts (raw)	100	4.9	1.6	36	550	1.5	—	29.0	390
Cabbage (raw)	100	0.9	0.8	34	90	0.3	1.5	13.0	163
Cauliflower	100	2.7	1.0	25	60	1.1	0.7	24.0	295
Celery (raw)	100	0.9	0.6	39	266	0.3	—	21.6	39
Collards (raw)	100	3.6	0.9	401	6,500	1.0	—	57.0	401
Corn (cooked)	100	3.2	0.7	163	396	3.0	—	20.0	163
Cress (raw)	100	3.0	1.0	610	9,300	1.0	—	12.0	610
Cucumber (raw)	100	0.9	0.6	25	245	1.1	0.1	11.2	158
Eggplant (raw)	100	1.2	0.9	12	10	0.7	—	16.0	214
Endive (raw)	100	1.8	0.9	82	3,000	1.8	0.2	10.0	294
Green Pepper (raw)	100	1.3	1.4	9	425	0.8	0.6	18.0	213
Kale (raw)	100	4.2	1.3	179	8,900	0.5	—	37.0	318
Mushrooms (raw)	100	2.7	0.8	6	5	0.8	12.0	10.8	406
Okra (raw)	100	2.4	1.0	249	520	0.6	—	41.0	249
Onion (raw)	100	1.5	0.6	27	41	0.5	1.5	11.8	155
Parsnips (raw)	100	1.7	2.0	50	30	0.7	—	32.0	541
Peas (raw)	100	6.3	2.0	26	632	1.9	—	34.5	311
Potato (raw)	100	2.2	0.8	7	5	0.6	—	—	409
Radish (raw)	100	1.0	0.7	28	5	1.0	4.2	14.0	290
Spinach (raw)	100	3.5	0.6	97	8,109	3.2	—	80.0	471
Sweet Potato (baked)	100	1.6	1.2	31	3,400	0.7	—	—	233
Tomato (raw)	100	1.1	0.5	16	905	0.6	0.5	14.1	245
Turnips (raw)	100	1.0	0.8	38	5	0.5	0.6	18.8	261

SOURCES: NUTRITIONAL ALMANAC and published scientific papers on cereal grass by Dr. George Kohler and others.

WHEAT GRASS IS A COMPLETE AND PERFECT FOOD

Wheat is the king of grains and has been known throughout history as "the staff of life." It contains every nutrient required by man, with the exception of vitamin D which is produced by the skin in conjunction with sunlight and cholesterol. Wheat grass perfectly mirrors the substances the human body needs to get from food. See the listing following this section.

THE MAKE UP OF WHEAT GRASS IS:

12% **WATER** – involved with nearly all body processes
70% **CARBOHYDRATES** – fuel supply
14% **PROTEIN** – builds tissue
2% **FAT** – supplies lubricant, protection and insulation
2.2% **FIBER** – helps with good elimination

The carbohydrate and protein content of wheat grass approaches the 80% to 20% ratio that is often recommended in truly healthy diets. Wheat grass contains pure vegetable protein "sans" the high cholesterol, additives and preservatives associated with protein obtained from meat. Wheat grass is an alkaline forming food due to its high percentage of carbohydrates and in particular to its calcium and potassium content. (The proper pH of the body is 7.35, which is slightly alkaline and maintained by alkaline forming foods). Another wonderful thing about wheat grass is that it does not contain gluten. Gluten is a substance many people have an allergic reaction to. However, it is only found in the kernel of wheat that develops if the cereal grass is not harvested.

IN ADDITION, WHEAT GRASS CONTAINS AN IMPRESSIVE ARRAY OF:

TRACE MINERALS – blood building/waste removal. If wheat grass is grown in mineral rich soil it is capable of absorbing almost all (103) of the 106 minerals known to man.

VITAMINS – growth and development of cells. In terms of vitamins, wheat grass has as much vitamin C as oranges and is higher in vitamin A than kale or collards. It is an excellent source of vitamin B including laetrile, which is an anti-cancer agent. B-12 is reputedly found only in meat but it is present in cereal grasses too. And vitamin K, difficult to reproduce artificially, is naturally occurring in wheat grass. It is needed for proper blood coagulation.

AMINO ACIDS – the raw building materials of protein. The amino acid content of wheat grass is so great that body builders take it as a protein supplement. It contains 17 of the 22 amino acids and all of the <u>eight essential ones</u> that the body cannot produce.

ENZYMES – workers that act as catalysts for carrying out thousands of chemical reactions in the body. Enzymes are essential to life. We are born with a certain innate amount of enzymes. Although our bodies can manufacture more enzymes they are constantly used up by dis-ease, age, stress and cooked, processed food. Over time we produce less and less enzymes so the body welcomes all the help it can get. When it comes to enzymes wheat grass is like "manna from heaven." In Hebrew "manna" translates into a surprise gift to man.

With regard to disease, wheat grass enzymes eliminate free radicals and are anti-aging. They also help with cell, organ and DNA repair and even have anti-cancer properties. From the perspective of food, enzymes ripen, producing the stages of growth from seed to plant to fruit. Each food carries it's own "designer enzymes" to digest it. Ingesting a food, such as wheat grass, in it's natural live state insures that this ripening or breaking down process will continue. The body benefits by not having to divert workers from other vital functions to aid in digestion and enzyme rich wheat grass adds to alkaline reserves necessary to maintain pH balance.

ELEMENTS FOUND IN WHEAT GRASS

MINERALS

CALCIUM
PHOSPHORUS
POTASSIUM
SULFUR
IRON
MAGNESIUM
SELENIUM
SODIUM
ZINC
IODINE
COPPER
COBALT
TRACE MINERALS

VITAMINS

BIOTIN
CHOLINE
FOLIC ACID
NIACIN
PATHOTHENIC ACID
PYRIDOXINE
RIBOFLAVIN
THAIMINE
VITAMIN A
VITAMIN B12
VITAMIN C
VITAMIN E
VITAMIN K

AMINO ACIDS

ALANINE
ARGININE
ASPARTIC ACID
GLUTAMIC ACID
GLYCINE
HISTIDINE
ISOLEUCINE
LEUCINE
LYSINE
METHIONINE
PHENYLALANINE
PROLINE
SERINE
THREONINE
TRYPTOPHAN
TYROSINE
VALINE

ENZYMES

AMYLASE
CATALASE
CYTOCHROME OXIDASE
LIPASE
PEROXIDASE
PROTEASE
SUPEROXIDE DISMUTASE
TRANSHYDROGENASE

THERE EXISTS A PHYSICAL, EMOTIONAL AND SPIRITUAL RELATIONSHIP BETWEEN PLANTS AND MAN.

On the **PHYSICAL** plane, a symbiotic relationship exists between man and plants. When we breathe in we take in oxygen and when we breathe out we give out carbon dioxide. Conversely, plants use carbon dioxide to synthesize air, soil and sunlight. As a by-product they give off oxygen.

EMOTIONALLY, we are in-tune with plants. Experiments show that plants, much like humans, are soothed by classical music but emotionally upset by acid rock. *The Secret Life of Plants* describe plants as growing to please us. They have even been used as human lie detectors.

SPIRITUALLY, plants are a marriage of physics and metaphysics. They are able to react to stimuli in their environment at a level of sophistication that far surpasses that of man. They are capable of intent, stretching towards and seeking out what they want in strange and mysterious ways. On a metaphysical level, plants have a way of communicating with the outer world that is far superior to our senses. The humble plant literally drinks in the universe and may just connect us to our maker.

Through this marriage of physics and metaphysics photosynthesis is produced. Plants harness the energy of the sun and store this harvest in the form of **CHLOROPHYLL.** This is an intelligent and amazing feat, again elevating plants over man in my estimation. We eat plants for this stored energy called chlorophyll. Chlorophyll is not a nutrient like protein, carbohydrates, amino acids and enzymes. Ronald L. Seibold, M.S. appropriately labels it as a food factor. While it is not essential to the diet of any animal it has been shown to be valuable and beneficial to humans.

The solid portion of wheat grass juice is 70% chlorophyll. It is the chlorophyll content of wheat grass that makes it such a powerful blood purifier. Chlorophyll has been described as the blood of plants and is remarkably similar to our own blood. It has the same pH balance as that of healthy human blood and it functions similarly, releasing oxygen in the air just as hemoglobin releases oxygen into human tissue.

The molecular structure of chlorophyll is only one ion different than that of hemoglobin. Chlorophyll has magnesium as its central atom while hemoglobin's is iron. A diagram of the molecular structure of hemin and chlorophyll is shown on the next page. These similarities were discovered back in the 1930's and scientists suspected that chlorophyll might be able to regenerate human blood. They were right. The human body is able to use chlorophyll as a substitute for the hemin pigment that combines with protein to form hemoglobin. In effect chlorophyll can rebuild the blood. It has been reported that within four to five days of taking wheat grass that red blood cell counts have returned to normal.

Billye Graham

The molecular structure of chlorophyll is only one ion different than that of hemoglobin. Chlorophyll has magnesium as its central atom while hemoglobin's is iron. A diagram of the molecular structure of hemin and chlorophyll is shown on the next page. These similarities were discovered back in the 1930's and scientists suspected that chlorophyll might be able to regenerate human blood. They were right. The human body is able to use chlorophyll as a substitute for the hemin pigment that combines with protein to form hemoglobin. In effect chlorophyll can rebuild the blood. It has been reported that within four to five days of taking wheat grass that red blood cell counts have returned to normal.

SIMILARITIES IN THE CHEMICAL STRUCTURES OF HEMIN AND CHLOROPHLL MOLECULES

HEMIN
(Oxygen carrying portion of Hemoglobin)

CHLOROPHYLL

The central atom of Hemin is Iron (Fe)

The central atom of Chlorophyll s Magnesium (Mg)

Billye Graham

HOW DOES WHEAT GRASS WORK?

IT NOURISHES

ENERGIZER

The starchy content of wheat grass is easily converted to simpler sugar, for energy and quickly absorbed into the blood stream. Less work is required to digest wheat grass since it is already broken down to food on a cellular level. This means more energy is available and less sleep required.

APPETITE DEPRESSANT

Wheat grass juice is far more concentrated than produce. One ounce of juice is equivalent to the vitamins, minerals and amino acids found in two pounds of green leafy vegetables. Once the cells are satiated, the appestat in the brain naturally shuts off. As a result less nourishment is required and you can begin to re-form the body by getting rid of fat and waste.

CLARITY OF THOUGHT

The high chlorophyll content acts as liquid oxygen. As more oxygen reaches the brain you will experience clarity of thought and purpose.

BLOOD BUILDER

Nutrients in wheat grass such as B12, folic acid, iron, copper, potassium and protein produce iron rich blood. Iron rich blood brings more oxygen to the cells. More oxygen increases the ability of cells to absorb nutrients.

DIGESTIVE AID

Wheat grass enzymes act as catalysts in the digestion of food and add valuable nutrients to alkaline reserves. Its vitamins, minerals and proteins are in their simplest forms minimizing digestion. It is synergistically proportioned to maximize assimilation and will enter the blood stream within twenty minutes of ingestion. It contains fiber and chlorophyll, which help to achieve and maintain colon health and regularity.

IT CLEANS

BLOOD PURIFIER

Chlorophyll combined with oxygen cleans foreign matter from the arterial walls and veins of blood vessels.

ANTISEPTIC – DEODERIZER

The cleansing properties of chlorophyll are good for dandruff, vaginal infections, sore throats, toothaches and decay, and skin ailments of all kinds. Given proper dietary habits, a prolonged intake of wheat grass will eliminate external body odors.

DETOXIFIES THE LIVER

Wheat grass cleans the liver, which in turn cleans the blood. The cleaner the blood the fewer germs and bacteria reach the cells.

COLON HEALTH

It cleans the colon walls of mucus allowing nutrients into the blood stream. Fiber content acts like a broom, sweeping the colon of debris, putrefaction and toxic buildup. It stimulates peristaltic action in the bowel to help with elimination and constipation.

STERILIZES

It sterilizes wounds, cuts and burns. Helps wash out drug and chemical deposits from the body. It is great for cleaning fruits and vegetables of insecticide sprays.

ENVIRONMENTALLY FRIENDLY

Biodegradable wheat grass containers are currently being manufactured to replace plastic ones. (Earth is a living breathing entity and landfills, full of non-biodegradable material, are a problem). Also adding wheat grass to fluoridated water (which is a poison) changes it into a healthy compound that is good for teeth and bones.

IT HEALS

DESTROYS DANGEROUS CHEMICALS

Wheat grass is one of the best sources of Beta-Carotene (Vitamin A).

Vitamin A, C and E are considered anti-oxidants that neutralize up to 80% of pollutants in air, water, food and soil.

ANTI – CANCER AGENT

OXYGEN - Dr. Warburg – German scientist – Nobel Prize – cancer cells cannot live in the presence of oxygen. Wheat grass is liquid oxygen.

ABSCICIS ACID – a plant hormone that prevents the germination of cancer cells and proves deadly to those already in proliferation.

LAETRIL – a substance that will selectively find and destroy abnormal growth such as cysts and tumors.

INDOLE – a tumor fighting substance.

IMPROVES CIRCULATION

Dilates blood vessels making them larger so that blood can flow through easier. Cleans blood vessels of arterial plaque giving relief from arteriosclerosis (hardening of the arteries), hypertension (high blood pressure by regulating blood sugar levels), Anemia (by adding iron to the blood) and arthritis (by dissolving calcium deposits). It increases metabolism, burns fat and produces weight loss. The enzyme D1-G1 has anti-inflammatory properties.

SKIN AILMENTS

Chlorophyll, and vitamin E content of wheat grass accelerates the restoration of connective tissue and heals ulcerated wounds and skin infections while minimizing scar tissue formation. It arrests the growth of unfriendly bacteria and reduces the side affects of radiation.

CELL REPAIR

DNA REPAIR – enzyme P4-D1 suppresses damage done to DNA molecules.

CELL REJUVINATION – root auxins regenerate damaged cells along with enzymes and amino acids.

ANTI – AGING – enzyme Super-oxide Dismutase slows down cellular aging by enabling cells to expel poisonous substances.

ORGAN REPAIR - will stimulate lymphatic system to move cellular waste out of the body and restore insulin production in the pancreas in cases of diabetes. Also stimulates the hearts vascular system, the intestines, the lungs and the sexual organs to perform their functions.

OTHER USES OF WHEAT GRASS

Outside of its medicinal properties lies a whole world of practical and beneficial uses of wheat grass. I have personally learned to incorporate wheat grass into my very being and in all that I do.

WHEAT GRASS IN THE KITCHEN

Fruits and vegetables contaminated by sprays can be cleansed with wheat grass. Wheat grass is a wonderful soak for non-organic vegetables to purge them of chemical fertilizers and pesticides.

FIGHT FATIGUE AND JET LAG WITH WHEAT GRASS

Wheat grass helps to ease the fatigue of jet lag by working with bio-rhythms and quickly resetting your biological clock. It also gets the pep back in your step with the energy it supplies.

SUSPECT AND CONTAMINATED WATER

One tablet of wheat grass added to a glass of water will neutralize the toxic effect of fluoridated water. It is the perfect way to enhance the quality of water encountered in one's travels and lessens the likelihood of getting Montezuma's Revenge (Diarrhea).

ANIMALS PREFER GRASS

Animals in the wild as well as our pets prefer grass when they are sick. During times of illness they will select a diet almost exclusively of grass even going without water. Adding wheat grass to their diet addresses health challenges from limps to lumps and everything in between. Give them wheat grass as a daily supplement (3 to 5 tablets or one liquid ounce). It provides extra-added energy and strengthens their immune system.

BODY BUILDING WITH WHEAT GRASS

Wheat grass contains 17 of 22 known amino acids, which are protein building blocks. Amino acids coupled with exercise, and weight training makes that six-pack chest and washboard stomach very obtainable.

PRIZE WINNING SCIENCE PROJECTS

My son attended Renaissance High School in Detroit, Michigan and was required to submit a science project his freshmen, sophomore and junior years. The only science I knew anything about was botany; composting and growing wheat grass. "A Comparison of Wheat Grass Growth in Composted versus Plain Potting Soil," took an honorable mention freshmen year. An idea had been born and we went on to do two more science projects with wheat grass. "The Effects of Colloidal Water (crystal treated) on the Growth of Wheat Grass" took Second Place sophomore year. And finally "The Effects of Magnetism on the Growth of Wheat Grass" took First Place in the All City Detroit Competition and 2nd Runner up for the Grand Prize in Botany for the State of Michigan Competition. Not bad for such humble beginnings with wheat grass being at the "root" of it all!

ROYAL BODY CARE

HAIR – helps eliminate dandruff. Rub juice into the scalp, rinse and shampoo. Makes hair squeaky clean and hides gray.

SKIN – tightens skin, stimulates growth of healthy new skin, applied topically improves varicose veins and sunspots. Also add to bath water for overall silky smoothness.

FEET – foot wash that soothes tired feet. The pulp is good for this.

EYES – excellent eye wash.

EARS – dip q-tip and swab ears.

MOUTH – excellent mouth wash that drains toxins from the gums and teeth (pyorrhea).

THROAT – Relieves sore throats – chew wheat grass blades ingesting liquid only. Discard pulp.

NOSE – an effective nasal rinse to open passages and contain nose bleeds.

FEMININE HYGIENE – dilute half and half with purified water and douche for vaginal infections.

FIRST AID – poultice for burns, ulcerated skin, boils, acne, infections, lacerations and puncture wounds. Can also apply liquid with cotton ball.

CHAPTER THREE

GREAT EXPECTATIONS

Billye Graham

YOU MAY HAVE A HEALING CRISIS

Wheat grass does not act like over the counter medicine that is designed to **SUPPRESS** troublesome aches and pains. Wheat grass balances the body both physically and emotionally and regulates bodily functions. This in turn stimulates the immune system to do its job. In fact, you may experience a temporary intensification of your physical crisis. Why is this?

In an attempt to keep major organs functioning, like the heart, the lungs and the liver, the body will store away toxins in secondary organs like the reproductive system and mammary glands (Breasts). When violations, which cause disease, are stopped and an environment conducive to health is implemented healing can take place. The body heals by taking toxic substances out of storage and eliminating them through **THE SKIN, BOWEL, LIVER, KIDNEYS, LUNGS** and **THE LYMPATHIC SYSTEM.**

HEALING is not the removal of symptoms it is the **REVERSAL OF DISEASE.** According to Homeopathy (a medical practice of opposites) the process of disease results from physical and mental imbalances brought on by trauma. <u>The direction of disease is from the outside in and from the bottom to the top.</u> This phenomenon is referred to as "Herring's Law of Cure" named after Constance

Herring (1800-1880) who was a leader in the American Homeopathic Movement. (1)

Consequently healing, the opposite of dis-ease, is a retracing process, going backwards in time. Healing recreates the same uncomfortable experiences we went through to produce disease. It is the elimination of these toxins that causes the dramatic symptoms of a healing crisis.

HOW DO I KNOW IT'S A HEALING CRISIS?

Sometimes it is difficult to tell the difference between a healing crisis and a new disease, making its first appearance. <u>But the direction of healing is always from the inside out and from the top to the bottom (Herring's Law of Cure).</u> Usually a **HEALING CRISIS** is precipitated by some sort of **LIFESTYLE CHANGE,** such as an improved diet, fasting, a new exercise regime or the cessation of unhealthy habits like smoking or drinking. The onset of a healing crisis is **SUDDEN** but **NOT LONG LASTING.** It generally lasts for several days to several weeks. A healing crisis is an **OUTPOURING OF TOXINS** (headaches, skin disruption, odors, and discharges) as opposed to internal pain or discomfort.

WHAT IS ACTUALLY HAPPENING?

The body is ridding itself of lower grade material and building with superior materials. This is a gradual process of breaking down and removing diseased cells and rebuilding healthy ones. First the quality of the blood improves creating stronger cells, tissues, organs and systems. Secondly, the eliminative organs are strengthened so that they are able to release the toxic build-up the body is mobilizing.

The healing crisis usually occurs at the peak of this house cleaning process. Outward signs, such as fever, headaches, chills, pain, nausea, vomiting, itching, rashes, diarrhea, sinusitis, discharges, earaches, dizziness, sweating, and heart palpitations, may be re-experienced.

Billye Graham

WHAT TO DO WHEN A HEALING CRISIS OCCURS

DO NOT ATTEMPT TO SUPPRESS THESE SYMPTOMS.

They are a part of the healing cycle though they may be unpleasant. Remember the symptoms are not the enemy it is the disease we are after.

TRY NOT TO PANIC during these cleansing periods. The greatest challenge is truly to not become discouraged. The inconvenience is temporary but the improvement is permanent! The best thing you can do is get out of the way of the body's efforts by:

1. **DRINKING WATER**

2. **RESTING OR DOING LIGHT EXERCISE**

3. **TAKING ENEMAS, IMPLANTS OR COLONICS**

4. **GENTLE BATHING**

5. **LIGHT FOOD, JUICES OR FASTING**

Realistically, a lifetime of accumulated toxicity will not be healed in short order and more than a few healing crises will have to be endured. **BE ENCOURAGED.** Healing is in progress and you are

**working towards your goal of good health with
every passing crisis. (4)**

WHAT TO DO AND EXPECT WHEN TAKING WHEAT GRASS

Billye Graham

HOW WHEAT GRASS TASTES

Wheat grass that is grown in composted soil, using earthworms is sweet to the taste and very palatable. Wheat grass that is grown outdoors is very strong and bitter to the taste. The chlorophyll content is greatly magnified from outdoor exposure to direct sunlight. Frozen wheat grass is less palatable than fresh. Sometimes you may be overwhelmed by the smell of wheat grass. During these times I resort to the use of tablets or rectal implants.

Billye Graham

WHEAT GRASS COMES IN DIFFERENT FORMS

Billye Graham

50

FRESH WHEAT GRASS

Fresh wheat grass juice is a powerful cleanser and may cause nausea shortly after ingesting. This is an immediate response to the release of toxins within the system. Take wheat grass on an empty stomach first thing in the morning. Start with small amounts such as 1 to 2 ounces of juice per day. Gradually work up to 3 to 4 ounces a day – 2 ounces twice daily. Single drinks of wheat grass larger than 3 ounces are not recommended because of the stirring effect this potent enzymatic juice has on the stomach and digestive organs.

Wheat grass is most powerful within 20 minutes of extracting the juice from the grass. However, it will retain its enzymatic properties for 10 to 24 hours provided that it is **kept refrigerated**.

Serious health challenges dictate that an earnest effort be made to drink wheat grass straight. It is not the most palatable juice so I will offer a few suggestions that may help to get and keep it down. **SMALL SIPS** on the tip of a teaspoon taken at intervals may help get wheat grass down. Also a **SLICE OF LIME** taken immediately after ingesting wheat grass makes a great chaser.

My favorite way to take wheat grass (on a maintenance basis) is a mixture I call <u>A WILD THING</u>: equal parts apple juice, pineapple juice, wheat grass juice and the juice of a lime to taste. COST: $1.25-$2.50 per ounce/$10-$15 per tray retail/ $6–$8 per tray wholesale.

51

FROZEN WHEAT GRASS

Frozen wheat grass is my least favorite form. It is not very palatable because freezing it changes the molecular structure and alters the taste. However freezing wheat grass does preserve the enzymes and prolongs the amount of time you can keep it on hand. COST: usually sold by the ounce(s) same costs as fresh.

FREEZE DRIED WHEAT GRASS

Freeze dried wheat grass can be added to salads or mixed with other juices or water. Sweet Wheat is a company that specializes in freeze-drying wheat grass in such a manner that the enzymes are preserved. (Sweet Wheat, Inc., P.O. Box 187, Clearwater, Florida, 33757, 1-888-227-9338, **WWW.sweetwheat.com**.

WHEAT GRASS TABLETS

When fresh wheat grass is not available, tablets work better for me. Take **no less than 7 tablets daily** and up to 10. Taking less than 7 tablets is not going to be effective as some of the enzymatic properties are lost in pill form. However, it will do the same thing as fresh wheat grass over time. Tablets are easy to swallow so you have no taste to worry about and the shelf life is indefinite. You can purchase tablets at local heath food stores ($7.95 for 100 tablets) or get larger quantities from wholesalers ($65.00 for 1500 tablets):

Pines International, P.O. Box 1107, Lawrence, Kansas, 66044, 1-800-697-4637, **WWW.wheatgrass.com.**

Pure Intentions Herb Farm, Attention: Kathy Evans, 162 North Portage Path, Akron, Ohio, 44303, 1-330-835-9463, e-mail: **pureintentions@hotmail.com.**

WHEAT GRASS IMPLANTS

A WHEAT GRASS IMPLANT is a good way to detoxify and revitalize the liver. An implant is a rectal insertion of the wheat grass juice. Wheat grass is delivered to the liver via the HEPATIC PORTAL SYSTEM. Tiny blood vessels called capillaries are attached to the small and large intestines. Nutrients from digested food pass directly through the colon walls to these capillaries. From there nutrients travel to the portal vein which in turn leads directly to the liver. THUS THE LIVER HAS THE FIRST OPPORTUNITY TO UTILIZE NUTRIENTS before passing the blood on through the inferior vena cava and into the rest of the blood stream.

The primary function of blood is to maintain a constant and healthy environment for the other living tissues in the body. Blood is the transportation system for foods, gases and wastes to and from the cells. The liver, the largest gland in the body, is primarily responsible for cleaning and regulating the blood. I think of the liver as a giant strainer. As the liver cleans the blood, fatty deposits and debris begin to clog its effectiveness. Wheat grass dissolves these deposits and re-establishes the proper cleaning of the blood.

There are three components in wheat grass that help the liver to stay vital and healthy:

CHOLINE–prevents fatty deposits that clog the liver

MAGNESIUM–draws out already existing fatty deposits

POTASSIUM–stimulates the liver to perform its tasks

Billye Graham

Cleaning the blood means fewer germs and bacteria are present that can reach the cells. And by the time the blood is clean, much of what ails us has simply disappeared!

IMPLANTS ARE DIFFERENT FROM ENEMAS AND COLONICS

Many people are confused about the difference between an implant, an enema and a colonic. An implant primarily cleans the lower bowel of large fecal matter while an enema and a colonic are extensive water treatments aimed at toning and cleansing the entire colon. One of the main objectives of these water treatments is to empty the <u>CECUM.</u>

The small intestines and the large intestines are joined together at the site of the ileo-cecal valve, the cecum and the appendix. If the food in the small intestines is toxic, a healthy appendix will not let it pass from the ileo-cecal valve into the cecum until it secretes a powerful neutralizing germicidal fluid. An unhealthy or removed appendix will permit a build up of toxicity in the cecum. It may take several colonics before the cecum actually empties as this signifies a through and complete cleansing of the colon. When the cecum empties, you will feel a warm sensation.

Implants, along with enemas and colonics fine-tune the colon, from the removal of large particles of debris to promoting peristaltic action to improving prolapsed conditions and evacuating parasites. To rebalance the flora and fauna (friendly bacteria) of the colon I suggest a non-dairy brand of <u>acidophilus</u> called DDS-1-Acidophilus with FOS. This product can be purchased at most health food stores.

(The cost is $16.95).

HOW TO TAKE AN IMPLANT

WHEAT GRASS STAINS- SOAK CLOTHING IMMEDIATELY

1. Use a 2-ounce baby syringe and implant 2-4 ounces of wheat grass – 2 ounces at a time.

2. Hold implant syringe in hand and squeeze out air.

3. Dip the end of syringe into freshly juiced wheat grass.

4. Let go of pressure on the bulb and wheat grass juice will be drawn into syringe.

5. To get air out of the bulb, turn full syringe tip up and squeeze out air. Dip back into wheat grass juice and release to draw up more juice into bulb.

6. Implant positions: insert while lying down on back with knees to chest or kneeling with chest to knees.

7. Insert tip into the rectum and squeeze tightly. Maintain pressure on the bulb until you draw the tip of the syringe from the

rectum. Once the bulb is out of the rectum release pressure on bulb and turn tip down. Reinsert into rectum and squeeze the rest of the juice into the colon.

8. Hold the implant for 20 minutes. To help in holding the implant lie down on bed or floor, put feet up against the wall or use a slant board.

9. If unable to hold the implant, release and immediately do another one. Implants stimulate peristaltic action in the colon. The second implant will cause a less intense reaction.

10. If the implant does not come out don't be alarmed. This is common. Part of the implant will be absorbed by the colon and transferred into the blood stream. The rest will be expelled with the next bowel movement.

CHAPTER FOUR

GENISIS/1:11

LET THE EARTH BRING FORTH GRASS!

Billye Graham

GROWING YOUR OWN WHEAT GRASS

SEEDS

Wheat grass is best grown from <u>hard red winter</u> wheat berries. This strain of wheat produces a high concentration of chlorophyll, active enzymes, vitamins, nutrients and amino acids. Soft wheat berries are less durable and do not yield equal nutritional value. Seeds can be purchased in smaller quantities from local health food stores ($1.69 pound) or in larger quantities (25lbs-50lbs) from wholesale seed catalog companies such as Harvest Time or Something Better in Michigan.

Harvest Time, 3565 Onandaga Road, Eaton Rapids, Michigan 48827, 1-800-628-8736. You will need to be affiliated with a health food organization (club or business). A minimum order of $35.00 is required. <u>WWW.harvestimenatural.com</u>.

Something Better Natural Foods, 22201 North-M66, Battle Creek, Michigan, 49017, 1-616-965-8500, <u>WWW.somthingbetternaturalfoods.com</u>.

SOIL

USE LOOSE LIGHTWEIGHT SOIL.

Non-Composted Soil. Mixture of 60% top-soil (good mineral source) 30% peat moss (good for root formation) and 10% vermiculite (good for drainage). Purchase at nursery or garden centers.

Canadian Sphagnum. A mixture of tree limbs, chips, moss and tree bark. Apartment dwellers may like this option. The mixture is lightweight, easy to carry, stores well in limited space and is odorless. Purchase at hardware, garden or nursery centers.

Composted Soil. My preference is composted soil because it's also nature's way! Be forewarned however, it is a lot of work! I use 39-gallon rubber made garbage cans with lids. Drill numerous small holes around the sides and bottom of cans for drainage. Purchase at any food chain, K-Mart or hardware store.

Layer compost as follows:
1. Upside down wheat grass mats (this is what's left after you cut the wheat grass at the roots from the soil. Turning it upside down helps to decompose it faster due to the lack of oxygen).

2. **Add wet shredded newspaper. (This adds and holds moisture).**

3. **Vegetable and fruit scraps - especially banana peels.**

4. **Red worms. (Earthworms can eat through all layers of this mixture and add valuable nutrients to the soil. You will need to replenish the earthworm population every year or two).**

Worms can be purchased at local bait shops or ordered by mail: Flowerfield Enterprises, 10332 Shaver Road, Kalamazoo, Michigan 49024, USA, 1-616-327-0108, WWW.wormwoman.com.

I take composted cans outside in the summer and inside in the winter (basement storage area). Composted soil may leak and have an odor due to decomposition. I personally do not turn the compost. The earthworms do a very good job by themselves. The mixture will need occasional water and air.

Hydrophonically.

Wheat grass can be grown hydrophonically (just water) without soil. Water contains mineral deposits, and minerals are what the grass picks up from the soil. (Vitamins come from the sunlight and photosynthesis). I prefer good old mother earth myself, but you may find this method convenient.

GROWING GRASS OUTDOORS

If you choose to grow wheat grass outdoors you should do it in high quality organic soil and in an open sunlit area. To improve existing soil add organic manure such as Malgranite. Grass grown in this manner reaches its nutritional peak in 30 days. Sprouting the seeds before planting greatly enhances the mineral and vitamin content of the grass. Water like any other garden vegetable.

Wheat grass grown outdoors has a bitter taste due to the high chlorophyll content obtained from direct sunlight. It is harder to juice than wheat grass grown indoors because the blades of grass are coarser. However, once the seeds are planted you do not have to work hard, only watering when necessary and you don't have a problem with mold from enclosure.

GROWING GRASS INDOORS

Growing grass indoors is a very labor-intensive process. It involves a lot of factors such as temperature, water, air, light, mold, insects, material requirements and a grow timetable.

Temperature

Wheat grass grows best in cool temperatures. Keep growing room temperature below 70 degrees.

Water

Use filtered water. Spring and distilled are also OK.

Air

You will need to open a window occasionally to let in fresh air.

Light

Use natural sunlight (sunroom or porch is good) or a grow lamp if grown in basement. I use my neighbor's spotlight at night, which is adjacent to my sunroom, and natural sunlight in the daytime.

Mold

Mold is natural since no pesticides or chemicals are used to control it. Rinse off regularly with water from a sprinkler can (use acidic water if available. It inhibits the proliferation of mold, which is bacteria).

Gnats

Decomposing material will naturally draw insects such as gnats and other flying insects. Sage plants will repel gnats. Also the use of pest strips is helpful. As a last resort I have been known to use an insect spray.

Material Requirements

1. Large wide mouthed glass jars for germination of seeds (4)

2. 6 to 10 school lunch trays for planting and covering wheat grass.

3. Garden tools – shovel/rake.

4. 2 to 4 rolling multi-level kitchen fruit & vegetable push carts.

5. A watering can with a sprinkler sprout. (A regular sprout pours too great of a concentration of water on the wheat grass tray). A sprinkler sprout gives you more control and even distribution.

6. Nylon mesh cut into squares large enough to cover the top of the glass jars.

7. Rubber bands to hold mesh screening in place over glass jars.

8. Pair of scissors to cut (harvest) wheat grass.

9. Large bowl to place cut wheat grass in.

10. Plastic ziploc bags to store harvested wheat grass in.

Billye Graham

TIMETABLE FOR GROWING WHEAT GRASS

Sprouting

Sprouting greatly enhances the nutritional content of wheat grass. It is like the difference between a bottle of soda pop and a bottle of champagne. One goes pop while the other one explodes. As a result of sprouting the vitamin and mineral content of wheat grass increases tremendously.

DAY 1

Place 1 cup of wheat berries in glass jar and cover ½ full with water. Cover glass jar with mesh screen and secure with a rubber band. Let soak in an upright position for 12 to 16 hours.

DAY 2

Drain the soak water off of the wheat berries. Rinse the seeds several times through the mesh screen being careful that it does not come off. Prop the jar in a secure setting at a 45-degree angle. Drain and rinse twice daily.

DAY 3

Repeat day 2 being sure to rinse twice daily. By day 3 the seeds should have little tails on them that show that they have germinated and sprouted.

DAY 4

Fill a tray even to the top with soil making small trenches around the edges to pour off access water. Spread the wheat berry seeds evenly on top of the soil so they are not clumped together or on top of each other. Water the soil and seeds with sprinkler can. The soil should be wet but not soaked. Cover with an additional tray. This simulates the normal growth conditions in nature.

DAY 5

Slightly raise the cover tray and check growth. If you find mold, uncover tray and lightly rinse off with sprinkler can.

DAY 6

The new growth of the wheat grass will be white to a pale yellow. The process of photosynthesis (harnessing sunlight) creates the green color of chlorophyll. Again check for mold.

DAY 7

Uncover the wheat grass tray. Place tray on multi-level pushcart and expose to direct sunlight. Water if necessary.

DAY 8 – 13

Water wheat grass tray as needed (when the soil feels slightly dry). Every other day to every two days should be good for watering. Don't over water as this will kill the roots and promote the growth of mold and fungus. Under watering will cause the grass to wilt.

DAY 14

Harvest wheat grass when the grass has reached 7 ½ inches or more. The yield varies between 6 to 10 ounces of wheat grass juice per tray.

Billye Graham

PROBLEM SOLVING

<u>My seeds failed to germinate.</u>
1. The seeds may be old. If unsuccessful on the second try then discard seeds.

2. Seeds that are soaked to long may not germinate. Water logged seeds destroy the root system. Follow sprouting instructions.

<u>My seeds are growing in the jar.</u>
1. You have sprouted the seeds too long. Sometime the seeds can be salvaged but it is usually best to start over.

2. Follow the sprouting timetable.

<u>Mold is growing on the wheat grass tray.</u>
1. Access mold can be the result of over watering or lack of air.
2. Use sprinkle type watering can and open windows routinely to circulate fresh air.

<u>My wheat grass is wilting.</u>
1. Wilting can result from a lack of water or too much heat. Wilting can also occur if the grass is allowed to grow too long.

2. Water when needed. Keep temperature in room under 70 and harvest when grass is 7 ½ inches in length.

<u>My wheat grass tastes mild or weak.</u>
1. An adequate amount of soil is necessary for root formation. Without adequate roots, the grass will not absorb ample nutrients from the soil. Also be sure to

use organic soil as other types may be depleted or lack mineral substance. (See section above on soil).

CHAPTER FIVE

WHEN ALL ELSE FAILS FOLLOW INSTRUCTIONS!

HARVESTING, STORAGE AND JUICING WHEAT GRASS

HOW TO HARVEST WHEAT GRASS

Take a pair of scissors and cut wheat grass close to the white part of the root, while holding the blade portion of the grass in your other hand. When cutting, grasp small to medium handfuls of grass at a time. If grass is moldy, at root, cut above the mold.

STORAGE OF HARVESTED WHEAT GRASS

Take a quart size zip lock bag and put a slightly moist paper towel in the bottom of the bag. Place grass with blades up and roots down towards towel to retain freshness and water source for roots. Prick holes in bag for airflow. Refrigerate but do not freeze. Use within 2 to 4 days of harvesting to retain enzymatic properties.

HOW TO JUICE WHEAT GRASS

It is not necessary to buy a wheat grass juicer. I was told of a lady who nursed her husband back to health by just getting him to chew the wheat grass blades. If you elect this method do not swallow the wheat grass pulp. Wheat grass is very fibrous and not very digestible. This is why you see animals, other than cows, regurgitate. Cows can swallow the grass because they have four stomachs to digest it.

Using a blender to chop wheat grass does not work very well. Wheat grass often clogs the blade and the resultant mixture is not finely chopped. The blender is also ill equipped to extract the juice.

A special wheat grass juicer is recommended. There are some inexpensive models available. (See following section on purchasing a wheat grass juicer).

Using a wheat grass juicer, place one cup under the juice spout and one cup under the pulp spout. Feed small handfuls of wheat grass into the juicer, blades down; it catches easier because the blades are thinner than the roots. The juice will come out of the bottom of the machine while the pulp will come out of the front on the juicer. (Save the pulp. See section on what to do with pulp).

STORAGE OF WHEAT GRASS JUICE

Pour into 1oz. or 2oz. plastic containers with lids. Wheat grass will oxidize rapidly and loose enzymatic properties within twenty minutes. If not consumed immediately freeze wheat grass juice. This will suspend the above-mentioned processes.

HOW TO UNTHAW WHEAT GRASS JUICE

To thaw wheat grass juice - 1) remove from freezer and place in refrigerator (24 hours) 2) thaw at room temperature (2 hours) 3) for rapid thawing place frozen container in a bowl of hot water (10 minutes).

WHAT CAN BE DONE WITH WHEAT GRASS PULP?

The pulp is very good for application to skin ailments. I use it in foot-baths along with white flour analgesic balm and find it totally relaxing and refreshing.

WHAT CAN BE DONE WITH THE WHEAT GRASS MAT?

The mat is excellent for composting or just enriching the soil in your yard. Pets really like wheat grass. Putting the mat outside and letting it re-grow for their use is another option.

Billye Graham

THINGS TO KNOW ABOUT WHEAT GRASS JUICERS

Wheat grass juicers are grinders fitted with a screen and a worm like extractor. The juicer is designed to turn slowly and press and squeeze the juice from grass. Regular vegetable juicers are not equipped to handle the fibrous nature of grass. They also tear and cut the product destroying enzymes from high speed processing.

What you will be looking for are juicers made out of CAST IRON with tin platting on the outside (to prevent rust) and STAINLESS STEEL screens on the inside. Wheat grass juicers made out of ALUMINUM are toxic and PLASTIC models do not hold up under rigorous use and break easily.

Both hand cranked and electric models are available. To extract more than one serving of juice, from a manual model is labor intensive and usually very tiring. However, manual models are less expensive than electric models and do a good job of juicing.

You will need to keep the wheat grass juicer clean. After each use disassemble parts and wash and rinse thoroughly. Before reassembling your juicer oil parts with a liquid vegetable oil. (Solid shortening tends to cake and spoil).

RECOMMENDED WHEAT GRASS JUICERS

The following juicers can be purchased from the Creative Health Institute, 112 W. Union Road, Union City Michigan, 49044, Phone: 517 278-6260, WWW.creativehealthusa.com.

WHEAT GRASS CHOPPER – Model 168671 - $50.00. Northern Industrial Tools, P.O. Box 1499, Burnsville, Minnesota, 55337, Phone: 1-800-533-5381, **WWW.northerntool.com.**

MIRACLE HAND HELD JUICER – Model MJ400 - $75.00. Miracle Exclusives, Inc., 64 Seaview Boulevard, Port Washington, N.Y. 11050, Phone 1-800-645-6360, **www.miracleexclusives.com.**

These are hand held juicers that requires some elbow grease to operate. They are metal and durable and the price is certainly right. They also do a good job of juicing the grass.

WHEATEENA LITTLE MARVEL – $300.00.
WHEATEENA CONVERTIBLE WORKHORSE- $560.00. Sundance Industries, P.O. Box 1446, 119 Broadway, Newburgh, N.Y., 12551, Phone: 1-914 565-6065, **WWW.noriv.com/sundance.**

An electric wheat grass juicer is best. The advantage is that you don't have to work so hard and you can juice large amounts of wheat grass at a time. The workhorse model can be converted from electric to manual.

Billye Graham

SAMPSON - $299.00
Greenbison, Inc., 2637 W. Woodland Drive, Anaheim, CA 92801, Phone: 1-888 992-7333, **www.sampsonjuicers.com.**

If you don't have a juicer of any kind, this would be a very good model to buy. It is a state of the art, six in one vegetable, fruit and wheat grass juicer.

CHAPTER SIX

**VALUE INFORMATION
TO CREATE
VALUE INFORMATION
TO TELL
VALUE INFORMATION
TO PLAN
VALUE INFORMATION
TO FOLLOW**

Billye Graham

GOOD QUESTIONS PEOPLE ASK ABOUT WHEAT GRASS

Invariably I will read a book then spend precious time trying to relocate important information or find the answers to questions. To assist you I have I have compiled a quick reference guide to commonly asked questions about wheat grass.

CAN I STILL TAKE WHEAT GRASS EVEN THOUGH I HAVE AN ALLERGY TO WHEAT? **Almost everyone who is allergic to wheat can take wheat grass. Gluten is the substance most people have an allergic reaction to. However, gluten is only found in the kernel of wheat that develops if the cereal grass (wheat grass) is not harvested. Mold that forms on stored wheat (again the kernel or grain) is another causative factor in wheat allergies. According to Dr. Donald Lepore, N.D., The Ultimate Healing System, allergies are caused by a deficiency of a certain nutrient or combination of nutrients that are necessary for the complete absorption of a particular food. In the case of wheat the missing nutrients are the mineral zinc, the amino acid histidine and safflower oil. Wheat grass contains two out of three of these antidotes so instead of aggravating the allergy it may in fact be helpful in correcting it.**

CAN I TAKE WHEAT GRASS ALONG WITH OTHER MEDICATION? **Yes you can. Wheat grass is a food not a medication. If you don't think twice about eating a large green leafy salad (which is the equivalent of 7 wheat grass tablets or 2 ounces of liquid wheat grass) when taking allopathic medications then don't worry about wheat grass. My father, a diabetic for 17 years took wheat grass tablets for two weeks and was told by** his doctor that his sugar was normal and he should stop taking insulin. You too may find that wheat grass is so helpful that you can stop medicating yourself. My sister, who had breast cancer took wheat grass before and after each chemotherapy treatment and survived the ravages of this procedure remarkably well. After four years she is still cancer free. So even if you elect allopathic treatments, wheat grass can strengthen your body and help it to weather these procedures.

ARE THERE ANY SIDE EFFECTS TO TAKING WHEAT GRASS? **No, there are no side effects to taking wheat grass. Medication alters the body's chemistry unnaturally and therefore creates an imbalance, which then gives rise to further problems and complications. Wheat grass triggers the immune system, which is the body's natural defense mechanism to do its job. You may experience a healing crisis, which is a perfectly normal response of the body in correcting imbalances. Healing is a process that requires you to walk back up the road of disease you followed to illness. This means that you will re-visit symptoms you manifested but didn't heed on your way back up. A healing crisis differs from the onset of a new disease in that it is sudden, usually do to a life style change; it does not last long, ranging from several days to several weeks; and characteristically it is an outpouring of toxins as opposed to an internalization of bacteria, viruses, parasites, etc.**

CAN TOO MUCH WHEAT GRASS BE TOXIC LIKE TOO MUCH VITAMIN A AND OR BETA CAROTENE? **Wheat grass juice has never been found to be toxic in any amount. Large quantities of wheat grass (over 2 ounces) consumed at one time can cause a lot of toxicity to flood the blood stream. This can result in nausea, weakness and dizziness. Unequivocally, you will not over dose on wheat grass.**

WHEN, HOW OFTEN AND HOW MUCH WHEAT GRASS SHOULD I TAKE AT ONE TIME? **Take wheat grass the first thing in the morning on an empty stomach so that it gets into the blood stream quickly and not held up with other foods through the process of digestion. Less is better than more. For adults, one to two ounces of wheat grass juice (or 7 tablets) per day is more than adequate to effect routine maintenance and promote good health. A health challenge may dictate an increase to twice daily the above dosage coupled with a wheat grass implant. Unlike allopathic medicine wheat grass stimulates the body's immune system and other bodily functions to correct imbalance (diseased states). Once this is accomplished you can return to daily maintenance or periodic administration.**

IS WHEAT GRASS SAFE FOR CHILDREN? **Certainly. Since their bodies are smaller and generally less toxic than adults a smaller serving of wheat grass is appropriate. You can start with one half to one ounce of liquid wheat grass (two to three tablets) on a maintenance basis and up to one ounce administered twice daily (two to three tablets twice daily) in case of illness or disease. Children over 12 can take adult dosages.**

WHAT IS THE DIFFERENCE BETWEEN WHEAT GRASS AND ORDINARY GRASS? **Wheat grass is soaked and sprouted before it is planted. This process increases its ability to absorb minerals from the soil and energy from the sun. Sprouted wheat grass seeds contain four times more folic acid and six times more Vitamin C then non-sprouted or regular grass seeds.**

WHY CAN'T WHEAT GRASS BE EATEN JUST THE WAY IT IS? **Wheat grass is very woody and fibrous and not at all suited for the long complex intestines of humans. Animals that graze on grass such as cows, horses, goats, hippopotamus's, etc. have short intestines.**

Cows actually have four stomachs, allowing them to chew, digest, regurgitate and re-chew the cud of grass. You too can chew wheat grass and still obtain amazing results. Just don't swallow the pulp.

WHY DO I NEED A SPECIAL JUICER TO JUICE WHEAT GRASS? The long thin structure of grass gets tangled in the blades of regular juicers and do not do a good job of extraction. Also regular juicers are not designed with powerful motors and can burn out. A hand held manual wheat grass juicer is relatively inexpensive, $35.00 to $50.00. An electric one certainly takes the work out of juicing wheat grass and is well worth the $250 to $300 investment.

WHAT IS THE BEST FORM OF TAKING WHEAT GRASS? Drinking freshly juiced enzyme rich wheat grass along with the synergy of its other nutrients is consuming it at its highest potency. Frozen, tablet and powder forms of wheat grass lose some enzymatic potency through processing but they all can produce equally beneficial results.

WHY IS IT THAT SOME WHEAT GRASS TASTES BITTER OR BLAND WHILE OTHERS TASTE SWEET? The difference in the varying tastes is due to the method of fertilization. Wheat grass fertilized with cow manure produces a bitter taste. Wheat grass grown hydrophonically (in water) or in a combination of substances other than soil lack minerals and produce a bland taste. I grow wheat grass like Mother Nature: in composted soil that is enriched by worm castings. It produces a very sweet palatable juice.

WHY DO I HAVE DIFFICULTY GETTING WHEAT GRASS DOWN AND WHY WON'T IT STAY DOWN? Difficulty in getting wheat grass down and the inability to keep it down suggests that the body is very toxic and unable to process the flood of toxicity flowing into the blood stream. I would recommend drinking wheat grass very slowly. Get a baby spoon and put just a little bit of wheat grass on the tip and sip it. You may even need to sip a little water in between. I once coached a lady through this process and it took over two hours for her to consume 2 ounces of wheat grass, but she kept it down.

OVER TIME, THE SMELL AND TASTE OF FRESH WHEAT GRASS CAN BECOME OVER POWERING. DO YOU HAVE ANY SUGGESTIONS FOR CONTINUED USE? **Yes. Do something different. Wheat grass tablets have no taste or odor. Sprinkle the powder on your salads or take an implant. Sometimes mixing wheat grass with other juices makes for a lively alternative.**

HOW ARE WHEAT GRASS TABLETS DIFFERENT FROM OTHER NUTRITONAL SUPPLEMENTS? **Most vitamin and mineral supplements are synthetically manufactured and not recognizable by the body. That is why 80% to 90% percent of it ends up in your urine as a very expensive shade of yellow. Wheat grass is a food containing naturally occurring vitamins and minerals easily recognized and readily usable by the body. You retain 80% to 90% of its benefits.**

HOW DOES WHEAT GRASS COMPARE TO OTHER SUPER FOODS? **There is no real nutritional difference that exists between one cereal grass and another. It really just boils down to a matter or taste. Some people prefer the super food Barley Green to Wheat Grass believing it to have a higher concentration of nutrients. Chlorella and Spirulina are also considered super foods. They are blue green algae (seaweed). They are known more for their protein content - 80% while cereals grasses (vegetables) are known for their carbohydrate content – 80%. Wheat grass mirrors the correct ratio of 80% carbohydrates to 20% protein** necessary to maintain the slightly alkaline pH balance of the body.

IF WHEAT GRASS IS SO BENEFICIAL THEN WHY AREN'T SCIENTISTS AND THE MEDICAL PROFESSION PROMOTING IT? **It was scientists and researchers who first discovered the benefits of cereal grasses added to the diet of farm animals. These findings have been documented over the last 60 years. It is not in the interest of large pharmaceutical companies or the American Medical Association to promote wheat grass. You must remember that illness is a business, healing is a p-r-o-c-e-s-s and health is a balanced state of mind body and spirit.**

INSTITUTIONS AND HEALTH PROFESSIONALS SPECIALIZING IN WHEAT GRASS THERAPY

The Wellness Center
Director: Mrs. Hiawatha Cromer
Health Retreat practicing the Living Foods Lifestyle
& Wheat Grass Therapy
Contact: (517) 663-1637-B
7881 Columbia Highway
Eaton Rapids, Michigan
48827
www.assemblyofyahweh.com/living.htm

Village of Natural Healing
Director: Mrs. Ada Cooper Robinson
Private Health Retreat practicing the Living Foods Lifestyle
& Wheat Grass Therapy
Contact: (616) 781-3010-B
14144 Verona Road
Marshall, Michigan
49068
E-Mail: village@internet1.net

Creative Health Institute
Director: Mr. Donald Haughey
Health Retreat Campus practicing the Living Foods Lifestyle
& Wheat Grass Therapy
Contact: (517) 278-6260-B
112 West Union City Road
www.creativehealthusa.com

Healing Support Network
Director: Mrs. Thelma Curtis
Macrobiotics, Living Foods Lifestyle & Wheat Grass
Contact: (313) 837-2414-B
16589 Strathmoor
Detroit, Michigan
48235
E-Mail: Hsn@velceroisp.com

Ann Wigmore Foundation
Health Retreat
Contact: (505) 552-0595-B
P.O. Box 399
San Fidel, New Mexico
87049
www.wigmore.org

Ann Wigmore Institute
Health Retreat
Contact: (787) 868-6307-B
P.O. Box 429
Rincon, Puerto Rico
00677
www.annwigmore.org

Optimum Health
Health Retreat
Contact: (619) 464-3346-B
6670 Central Avenue
Lemon Grove, California
91945
www.optimumhealth.org

Hippocrates Health Institute
Health Retreat
Contact: (561) 471-8876-B
1443 Palmdale Court
West Palm Beach, Florida
33411
www.hippocratesinst.com

Billye Graham

BIBLIOGRAPHY

ARTICLES

1.   Bier, Deborah, "Understanding Healing Crises," East West Journal, January 1988, Page 16.

2.   CREATIVE HEALTH INSTITUTE, The Wheat Grass Place, 112. West Union City Road, Union City, Michigan 49094. Dalmia, Yashodhara, "Health from Grass – Wheat Grass the Cure All?" Licata, Vincent, "Chlorophyll: Nature's Green Magic."
"Some Things We Learned About Wheat Grass."
"The Wonders of Wheat Grass."
"Uses of Wheat Grass Juice for the Body."
"What Are the Benefits of Drinking Wheat Grass?"

3.   EDEN FOODS, 701 Tecumseh Road, Clinton, Michigan, 48236.
"Transition Period from Previous Habits to a New Dietary Practice."

4.   Grauwels, Marlene, P.O. Box 70, Fairchild, Wisconsin, 54741-0070.
"How to Aid the Body to get the Best Results from a Healing Crisis."
"Are You Sick or are you Cleansing?"
"Understanding the Benefits of Detoxification."

5.   Gross, Lou, Natural Health Consultant, "Incorporating Healing Grasses into your Diet." Healing Garden Journal, November 2001, Page 17.

6. Krasen, Bill, **"Nutritionist, Author Supports the Start of a Time of Caring,"** Kalamazoo Gazette, **Monday, July 30, 1990.**

7. Monte, Tom, **"Steps to Health-What we can Learn from People who've Made Amazing Recoveries from Terminal Illnesses," East West Journal, June 1995, Page 4.**

8. Perfect Food, Inc., **"Green Gold Wheat grass Juice,"** New York, N.Y. **Harley Matsel & Jack Mevorah (1-800-933-3288).**

9. Pines Wheat Grass, **Box 1107, Lawrence, Kansas, 66044.**
"What is the Difference between Wheat Grass and Green Barley?"
"When Does Wheat Grass reach its Peak in Nutrition?"
"Wheat Allergies and Wheat Grass."
"Wheat Grass for Endurance."

10. Pookrum, Jewel, **Civilized Medicine Institute, Atlanta, Georgia.**
"Be prepared to experience what is known as the Healing Crisis."

11. Rays from the Rose Cross, **"Wheat grass Super food?" 2222 Mission Avenue, Oceanside, California, 92054, Volume 88, 1996, Page 228.**

12. Rossof, Michael, **"The Healing Road: Natural Cycles to Health," Macromuse, Autumn/Metal 1986, Page 6.**

13. Sweet Wheat, **Inc., P.O. Box 187, Clearwater Florida, 33757.**
"Top Ten Questions and Answers on the Wonders of Wheat Grass Juice."
"Wheat Grass Juice – A Healing Aid."

14. Walker, Dr. Morton, "**The Sweet Wheat way to Optimal Nourishment**," Explore, Volume 8, Number 4, **1998.**

BOOKS

15. Kreucher, Dr. Robert A. ***Harmonious Healing,*** **Ann Arbor, Michigan, Colossos Printing, 1998.**

16. Melody, ***Love is in the Earth,*** **Wheat Ridge, Colorado, Earth-Love Publishing House, 1995.**

17. Meyerowitz, Steve, ***Wheat Grass, Natures Finest Medicine,*** **Great Barrington, Massachusetts, The Sprout House, Inc., 1991.**

18. Seibold, Ronald L. M.S., ***Cereal Grass,*** **New Canaan, Connecticut, Keats Publishing, 1991.**

19. Smith, Li, ***Wheat Grass: Super Food for a New Millennium,*** **Bloomingdale, Illinois, Vital Health Publishing, 2000.**

20. Tompkins, Peter & Bird, Christopher, ***The Secret Life of Plants,*** **New York, N.Y., Harper & Row Publishers, 1973.**

21. Wigmore, Ann, ***The Sprouting Book,*** **1986, The Wheat Grass Book, 1985, Why Suffer, 1985, Wayne, New Jersey, Avery Publishing Group.**

MEDICAL RESOURCES

22. Burney, Leroy, *Medical Aid Encyclopedia for the Home*, Nashville, Tennessee, Royal Publishers, Inc., 1978. (Cecum pg. 109, glands pg. 265, portal vein pg. 406).

23. Chabner, Dave & Ellen, *The Language of Medicine*, Philadelphia, Pennsylvania, Harcourt Brace and Company, 1976. (Hepatic portal system pg. 134, 137, 346-349, 431).

24. Cohen, Alan, *The Dragon Doesn't Live Here Anymore*, New York, N.Y., Fawcett Books, 1993.

25. *Dorlan's Pocket Medical Dictionary*, Philadelphia, Pennsylvania, Harcourt Brace and Company, 1982, 24th Edition. (Porta/portal pg. 483).

26. Gray, Henry, *Gray's Anatomy*, Philadelphia, Pennsylvania, Running Press, 1974. (The liver page 933. The portal system of veins pg. 619-621).

RESEARCH DONE ON WHEAT GRASS

27. "A Scientific Appraisal of Dr. Ann Wigmore's Living Food Lifestyle," Boston, Massachusetts, Ann Wigmore Press, 1993.

28. Lai, Dr. Chui-Nan, **Global Healing Information Service Network, P.O. Box 1795, Soquel, California, 95073, 1-415-591-1145.**

PART II:

TO SOUL

Billye Graham

CHAPTER SEVEN

ILLNESS IS A BUSINESS$$

HEALING IS A P-R-O-C-E-S-S!!

HEALTH IS A BALANCED
STATE
OF
MIND, BODY AND SPIRIT

Billye Graham

A NEW START

By all means, do consult a doctor when you are faced with a HEALTH CHALLENGE. There are life-threatening situations that call for immediate attention and immediate action. Wheat grass is preventative therapy and curative over time. Wheat grass as the cornerstone of any health challenge can do much but a holistic approach to health and healing requires obedience to all of nature's laws.

Many of us need to start anew in pursuit of health. A NEW START is a fresh opportunity to review our physical health, examine our knowledge of the natural laws that govern health and healing and make any changes in the way we think and eat in order to become HEALTHIER HAPPIER BEINGS.

A N-E-W S-T-A-R-T is an acronym for A WELLNESS SOLUTION:

ATTITUDE

NUTRITON
EXERCISE
WATER

SUNSHINE
TEMPERANCE
AIR
REST
THOUGHT

Affirming these **KEY PRINCIPLES** that define **HEALTH** incorporates them into our consciousness until they become a part of our very being. **AFFIRMATIONS** are positive statements that we repeat over and over again. The human brain is like a blank record or computer disc. When we repeat these positive statements for 30 days or more it makes an indelible impression on the mind and changes "our tune" so to speak. Affirmations are our food for thought. They contribute to our mental well being as much as food contributes to our physical well being.

<u>**The quality of our lives is in direct proportion to our understanding and willingness to practice these immutable laws:**</u>

ATTITUDE – YOUR APPROACH TO LIFE

Every crisis is an opportunity to do something different. I was grateful to the universe for my health challenge. Many people never get the blessing of a warning. Instead of the negative connotation of disease, refer to your crisis as a HEALTH CHALLENGE. Challenges provide positive motivation in changing thoughts and behavior.
AFFIRMATION: <u>**I HAVE AN ATTITUDE OF GRATITUDE**</u>.

NUTRITION – THE NOURISHMENT OF LIFE

Life comes from life. Life is sustained by food that is:

<u>Living</u>

Still growing like sprouts or fermented foods teaming with live lacto-bacillus (friendly bacteria)
Or raw foods that still contain the life force and are able to reproduce in kind such as fruits and vegetables

Properly combined

Liquids alone
Melons alone
Fruits alone
Acid fruits or sweet fruits with sub-acid fruits
Complex carbohydrates or proteins with green leafy vegetables

Properly digested

Chewing to reduce food to small particles
Break down of food-churning action of stomach with enzymes

Properly Assimilated

Nutrients pass through the wall of the small intestines

Properly Eliminated

Waste passes from the lymph and through the bowel, kidneys, lungs and skin.

Periodic and Seasonal Cleansing of the Digestive Track

Fasting –Three days for cleansing – one day for maintenance
Wheat grass Implants or Colonic Irrigations with water.
AFFIRMATION: I EAT TO LIVE NOT LIVE TO EAT.

Exercise – Staying Fit for Life

Food is married to exercise. Food provides the fuel and exercise burns the fuel to create energy. They take **C. A. R. E.** of each other and you too in the process.

Circulates – exercise increases the blood flow & circulates nutrients

Assimilates – exercise breaks down food & helps assimilate it

Rejuvenates – exercise oxygenates the blood & facilitates cleansing

Eliminates – exercise activates the lymph & colon peristalsis

Best Impact Exercises:

Walking, Tai Chi and Yoga

Best Non-Impact Exercises:

Water Aerobics, Trampoline and the Chi Machine
AFFIRMATION: <u>I EXERCISE MY RIGHT TO BE FIT.</u>

Water – The Elexir of Life

Our make up is two-thirds water and it only makes sense that we consume, in large portion, what we are. Water cleanses, bathes and refreshes. It is necessary to carry out important bodily functions. A pure source of water is vital to health.

Recommended:

Spring Water contains minerals
Distilled Water (in moderation-short run- leach out free radicals over time-leach out minerals – add trace minerals)
Reverse Osmosis – removes particles, odors, bacteria
Ionized Water – electrically charged alkaline water that allows cells to absorb more nutrients from consumed food
AFFIRMATION: <u>I QUENCH MY THIRST FOR LIFE WITH PURE CLEAN WATER.</u>

SUNSHINE – THE ENERGY OF LIFE

All that exists on earth does so because of the energy provided by the sun. Without sunlight plants cannot harvest this energy and supply our daily needs for it. We also need at least fifteen minutes daily of direct exposure to sunlight. When the sun irradiates cholesterol in the skin it is converted into vitamin D. Vitamin D is an essential fat-soluble food substance affecting the calcium and phosphorus content of body fluids. We are much less aware that our eyes use basic nutritional food (light) to bring about health. The eyes are the major access routes by which light enters the body and there is a connection between the eyes and the brain. Light entering the body through the eyes goes directly to the hypothalamus, which monitors light-related information. The hypothalamus controls the nervous system and endocrine system, whose combined effect regulates all biological functions in the body. And last but not least the emotional affect of penetrating sunrays is cleansing and its rainbow effect evokes happiness and well-being.
AFFIRMATION: <u>YOU ARE THE SUNSHINE OF MY LIFE.</u>

Temperance – THE MAINTENANCE OF LIFE

There is an art to staying alive and "quality living:" **SIMPLICITY.**

Temper your thoughts, work habits, food intake, drink and merriment with purity and moderation in all things. All natural occurring herbs and substances have some universal purpose and many have medicinal properties, i.e., opiates sedate, derivatives of the cacao family stimulate, alcohol anesthetizes pain, marijuana is used to treat glaucoma, an eye disease and even tobacco was used by native Americans to cook with in beans and cure a range of ailments including constipation, bleeding gums, upset stomach and headaches. The point is Mother Nature did not intend these substances for sport.

AFFIRMATION: <u>I LIVE SIMPLY SO THAT OTHERS MAY SIMPLY LIVE.</u>

Air – THE BREATH OF LIFE

Air or oxygen is by far the single most important component of life as we can only live a few minutes without it. All a cell needs to sustain life is air and water (liquid oxygen). While we often look outside of ourselves for calming agents, nature has given us a built-in STRESS BUSTER – **DEEP BREATHING.** Breathing in through the nose, to the count of five and out through the mouth, to the count of five will calm you down. (Repeat five times). Also opposite nostril breathing will actually lower your blood pressure. Hold the right nostril and breath in through the left. Exhale through the right. Hold the left nostril and breath in through the right. Exhale through the left. (Reverse and repeat five times).

AFFIRMATION: <u>I BREATHE DEEPLY IN APPRECIATION FOR THE LIFE GIVING PROPERTIES OF AIR.</u>

Rest – THE RENEWAL OF LIFE

Rest at least four to six hours a day. Rest restores our physical energy and our mental clarity. Anything that does not rest will soon wear out. Even God rested on the seventh day of creation from labor. Life's silver lining comes from fun, experiencing joy and resting in appreciation of what you have created and accomplished. All work and no play will not complete your life and affairs. When it's all said and done someone else will.

AFFIRMATION: I GIVE MYSELF PERMISSION TO REST AND BUILD RELAXATION INTO MY DAILY ROUTINE.

Thoughts – THE CREATION OF LIFE

Thoughts are things that create. Words are things that manifest. And what we dwell or focus on gives it the right to live within us and emanate from us. The body follows the mind. Think it and so shall it be. We cultivate good thoughts by **PRAYING** (asking God for guidance) and **MEDITATING** (listening to God for the answers).

AFFIRMATON: I THINK GOOD THOUGHTS AND MY EVERY WORD IS A PRAYER OF PRAISE AND THANKS-GIVING.

IN SUMMATION

Utilize A N-E-W S-T-A-R-T to activate a life style change. And utilize affirmations to transcend and re-program outdated attitudes and behavior patterns. Pursue new ideas. Accentuate the positive. Cultivate healthy habits. Find and learn the lesson. Grow spiritually. Couple all of this with Wheat Grass Therapy and you have the ingredients of a balanced, health-filled, life enhancing combination.

Billye Graham

EPILOGUE

I would like to give credit for the concept of A New Start to Ms. Dorothy Brunson of Denver, Colorado. She is a Herbologist, Reflexologist and Massage therapist and gives Friday seminars and family health weekends. **(WWW.DBHerbes.com).** Some years ago I attended a lecture she gave in Lansing, Michigan and became enthralled with the idea of starting anew and being born again through health. I have incorporated it into my every thought as it very simplistically explains the basic tenets, doctrines and laws of health.

Billye Graham

CHAPTER EIGHT

Healing Vibrations Are Good vibes

Billye Graham

VIBRATIONAL THERAPY

Due to the growth of Alternative Medicine the idea of man, as a physical being only, treated by drugs and surgery, has begun to change. The Holistic approach to wellness embraced by alternative health practioners encompasses our physical mental and emotional make-up. And more recently Vibrational Therapy further defines the body as an energy vibration.

Dr. Richard Gerber, M.D. author of *Vibrational Medicine for the 21st Century,* writes "illness is thought to be caused not only by germs, chemical toxins and physical trauma but also by chronic dysfunctional emotional-energy patterns and unhealthy ways of relating to ourselves and other people. Rather than relying on drugs and scalpels, vibrational therapy utilizes love (the highest vibration of all) coupled with many different forms of energy enhancement to bring about healing."

Everything in the universe is energy and all energy vibrates. There are many types of energy that make up the electromagnetic spectrum providing healing vibrations through our seven senses: hearing-sound, seeing-light, smelling-spiritual scent, tasting-physical smelling, feeling-physical touch and sensing-spiritual feeling. We often overlook the fact that we are surrounded by an electromagnetic field that is an integral part of our sensibilities. The only difference between these forms of energy is that each moves at a different frequency or rate of vibration.

John & Lucie Davidson, *Harmony of Science and Nature*, describe the cause of this motion as polarity and duality. "Even solid and stationary objects are no more than vibrating energy fields of positive and negative electrical charges gravitating between north and south magnetic fields. Motion exists because of this inequality. Energy in its eternal cosmic dance seeks a state of balance: high moves to low, positive runs to negative, clockwise is balanced by anti-clockwise and as it moves, it experiences a force pulling it back to where it was and so it vibrates, orbits or oscillates."

I define a vibration as the speed at which something thrives or changes its energy form. All vibrations can be tuned to their correct frequencies or raised to a level that changes them. The most familiar example of this is water. When it is heated it turns to steam and when it is frozen it turns to ice. Music also provides some good examples. Almost everyone is familiar with the Memorex commercials in which the high-pitched sound of a human voice shatters glass. It has been well documented that plants thrive on classical music while acid rock can literally whither them. Even the walls of Jericho, by biblical account, came tumbling down from the blasts of trumpets built up to a tremendous vibration.

Vibrations affect all processes of life, including healing. Healing, in terms of vibrations, simply means restoring harmony between the energy patterns of the human constitution. John & Lucie Davidson identify three subtle energy patterns or circuits in the body along with what drives them:

The Mental Circuit controls the brain, the head and the main sense organs, the throat and speech. It is particularly strong in intellectual and highly rational people.

The Emotional Circuit controls the heart, lungs, liver, kidneys, spleen and solar plexus. The energy that manifests here is derived from feelings and emotional expression.

The Physical Circuit controls the pelvic area including the sex organs, the legs and the hands. It is usually the most powerful energy present in physically oriented people.

All energy (vibrations) is interconnected, between human beings, our immediate environment and the cosmos. Let us consider vibration therapies that assist healing and relate to wheat grass therapy.

SCENT

The therapeutic benefits of **Aromatherapy** (plant essence) are heightened when natural essential oils of the highest quality are used. **Essential oils** have clean aromas that evoke recognition, association and memories. They act directly on the olfactory nerves of the brain either stimulating or relaxing them. Also when applied to the skin essential oils can be very beneficial. The skin is an organ that is capable of accepting nourishment as well as releasing toxins. Edgar Cayce popularized the use of castor oil as a detoxifying agent for the liver, gallbladder and digestive system when applied topically as a warm pack.

SENSE

All animals are endowed with **instinct**. Instinct has to do with elements that enter our spatial perception. We have all experienced the sense that we are not alone when indeed someone has entered a room behind us and permeated our space. We are all surrounded by auras that interact when we are in each other's presence. This explains how other people's moods can similarly affect us. Husbands and wives who live together for many years can take on very similar features in both physical appearance and mental and emotional attitudes. They are living within each other's aura. Their vibrations have become attuned to each other. This partially explains why one spouse will follow the other in transition within days or months of each other.

FEELING

Dr. Edward Bach of England made the startling discovery of a medical connection between feelings and actual physical illness: "inharmonious states of mind nearly always accompanies dis-ease and may in fact be it's primary cause." Throughout the 1920's and 1930's he developed thirty-eight remedies known collectively as **The Bach Flower Remedies**. They were made from wild plants, flowers, bushes or trees. They were not intended for physical complaints but were used to affect a patient's mental state of mind. Dr. Bach did not offer any scientific explanation for why Bach Flower Remedies worked but many clients and holistic practioners have sung their praises over the years, including me. In many case studies they resolved the problem when all else failed because these remedies treat the patient and not the dis-ease.

TASTE

Taste can make you spit something out with vehemence or delight the pallet to no end. The esthetics of food and drink either agree or disagree with us depending on their vibrations. Foods that contain **chlorophyll**, followed by bright colors, have a higher vibratory rate than other foods. Also **living and raw foods** have a **higher vibration** than cooked, altered and processed food.

MAGNETISM

A magnet has two sides north and south corresponding respectively to the magnetism of the North Pole and South Pole. When applied to a biological system north and south pole magnetism produce different effects. **North pole (negative)** energy tends to **pull things together** causing contraction. **South Pole (positive)** energy tends to cause things to expand and thereby **dissipate**. Many diseases have been successfully treated with magnetism. Donald Lepore, N.D. *The Ultimate Healing System* reports that magnetism has been used to arrest certain diseases such as cancer, in laboratory rats. Arthritis has been improved through the use of North Pole energies and tumors and growths have been shrunk through the use of South Pole energies.

ELECTRICAL CURRENT

In 1933 Royal Raymond Rife discovered that **viruses** and **bacteria** were easily **destroyed at low-level energy currents**. He developed the **Rife Machine** that was able to identify the electronic signature of specific diseases. It was used successfully to help many people recover from cancer. However, Rife's technology was actively opposed by the American Medical Association. Its use was banned for many years in the United States. Interest returned in the Rife Machine with the publication of **The Cancer Cure**, by Barry Lynes in 1987. Today this technology is actively promoted by John Wright Laboratories.

In Ruth Montgomery's *Born to Heal*, she speaks of a remarkable healer whom she referred to as Mr. A. Although he was not a doctor he was much sought after to perform what he called "**electrical tune-ups**."

Mr. A deemed "the life force" electrical energy. According to him our bodies are mechanically constructed to conduct and transmit this energy through the magnetic field that surrounds it. The control center for the magnetic field is located in the lower abdomen. Each person's surrounding energy is as individual as fingerprints. He was able to perceive where there was weak energy then match an individuals wave lengths and frequencies, thereby energizing and correcting ailments in a matter of minutes.

OSCILLATING FREQUENCY

In the 1990's Dr. Zhizou Inoue of Japan developed an energy-enhancing device called a <u>Chi Machine</u>. Chi is the Chinese word for "the life force." They believe that chi is extracted from the food we eat and aids in the formation of our blood, which carries it to our organs and tissues. Chi can only be used properly if our acupuncture-meridian system is free from blockages or energy imbalances. The Chi machine duplicates the <u>oxygenating and energizing effects</u> of the figure-eight movement of fish. By oscillating at a parti-cular rate within a well-defined range of motion this machine raises the vibrational level of the body through increased oxygenation of the blood, improved circulation, deep breathing, balancing the left and right hemisphere of the brain, relaxing the spinal cord and calming the autonomic nervous system.

SOUND

Sharry Edwards created the field of Sound Therapy called **Bio Acoustics** which means "life sounds." She has the unusual ability to hear beyond the normal human range of 20-20,000 cycles per second. Her ability coupled with research has substantiated that each human being emits silent sounds that correspond to musical notes. (See Charkas Chart that follows). These individualized frequencies, called **"signature sounds,"** are a combination of genetic coding, geographic locale, brain and neural functions, biochemistry, emotions, physical structure and environmental influences.

Using Bio Acoustics, the state of your health can be determined from the sound of your voice. When frequencies of the body become distorted, demonstrated through pain or emotional stress, a voice-print will be able to display these distortions as stressed or missing frequencies. When these missing sounds are returned to the environment the body begins to stabilize, strengthen and rebuild it self, even from so-called incurable dis-eases.

Bio Acoustics has assisted in recovery treatments such as arthritis, emphysema, epilepsy, heart problems, gout, high blood pressure, mental retardation, multiple sclerosis, Lou Gehrig's disease, bone integrity, genetic syndromes, environmental allergies, metal toxicity, structural muscle damage, chronic pain, Down's syndrome and attention deficit disorder (ADD).

LIGHT – COLOR THERAPY

While there are many forms of light therapy, the focal point of this discussion will be on **Color Therapy**. Color is a powerful vibrational stimulus. It gives off waves of electromagnetic energy that is constantly transmitted to the eye and brain affecting human moods, behavior and perception.

Your personality can be revealed through your preference for colors. I once had a color preference analysis done by Potential Unlimited, Inc. I was simply amazed at how accurate the analysis was about my attitudes, needs, abilities and difficulties in life.

Color can make our figures appear more perfect than they actually are through optical illusion. Color Me A Season Educational Color Corporation teaches how to dress with color. Use stronger more intense colors for the pleasing aspects of your figure while employing darker, less vibrant colors to draw attention away from less flattering areas.

You can even change your mood with color therapy. Terri Perrigone-Messer, designer of Color Therapy Eyewear says just slip on a pair of her rose colored glasses and say goodbye to aches and pains. These therapeutic glasses can get rid of a migraine-red, spice up your sex life-orange, calm your nerves-green, get rid of allergies-blue, wise you up-purple and help you lose weight-yellow.

The human body is literally fed by sunlight, which is made up of a rainbow of colors. <u>Color is a natural healer</u> working it's magic through vibration. The three primary colors are red-physical, yellow-mental and blue-spiritual. Since this book is about wheat grass I am going to concentrate on the color green. <u>Green</u> is a combination of blue and yellow, a balance between the spiritual and the mental, necessary to stimulate the physical aspect of healing. Thus in color therapy GREEN <u>is associated with healing:</u>

MENTALLY – green balances perception and action

PHYSICALLY – green energizes, cleans and heals

EMOTIONALLY – green calms, soothes and harmonizes

SPIRITUALLY- green promotes change, growth and maturation

Just as our bodies crave certain foods when we are out of sync, the body craves certain colors for restoration of balance. Energy patterns, which flow through the <u>chakras (energy points on the body</u>), sometimes get interrupted causing the wheels of the charkas to spin erratically or shut down completely resulting in energy blocks. Each color vibrates at a specific frequency as do the glands and organs along the bodies chakras. Matching colors to energy points re-balances trapped energy and can bring in higher energy patterns.

The seven energy charkas, line up down the center of the body (See Chart). As you can see **HEALING GREEN** is associated with the **4th or Heart Chakra**. It is the center of the love vibration, requiring a delicate balance of harmony, compassion and forgiveness to remain open and unobstructed.

The Heart's Code, by Paul Pearsall, M.D., makes a powerful case for the heart being the seat of the soul. He relates remarkable stories by heart transplant recipients who have changed their food preferences and personalities along with having dreams and fantasies related to cellular memories of their donors. He even recounts a story of one young heart recipient who was able to identify the murderer of her heart donor. It may very well be that the heart indeed contains the seed atom of our cellular memories.

CHAKRA POINTS

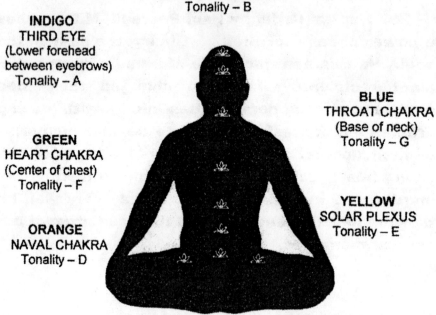

VIOLET
CROWN CHAKRA
(Center top of head)
Tonality – B

INDIGO
THIRD EYE
(Lower forehead
between eyebrows)
Tonality – A

BLUE
THROAT CHAKRA
(Base of neck)
Tonality – G

GREEN
HEART CHAKRA
(Center of chest)
Tonality – F

YELLOW
SOLAR PLEXUS
Tonality – E

ORANGE
NAVAL CHAKRA
Tonality – D

RED
SEXUAL CHAKRA
(Groin points)
Tonality – C

The heart chakra is located in the center of the chest and is considered a neutral point falling between the three lower energy centers with their warming colors of red, orange and yellow and the three higher energy centers with their cooling colors of blue, purple and violet. The lower chakras relate to personal love while the higher ones relate to universal love. The heart chakra is a balance point. When it is wounded by hurt or betrayal its energy flow can become interrupted as well as block the energy flow to the third-small intestines and fifth-throat charkas. Food doesn't get digested and a feeling of suffocation can accompany these blockages.

CRYSTAL THERAPY

When the heart is wounded it needs opening to let in love-light energy. Holistic practioners versed in Crystal Therapy will use this <u>amplifying energy</u> to accomplish this task. Crystals abound in everyday usage, i.e., quartz watches, laser surgery, micro-chips, fiber optics, etc. But few know that crystals are actually inherent in the human body.

Dr. Alex Carrell won the Nobel Prize in Medicine for demonstrating that the cells of our bodies are virtually designed for immortality. He discovered that it was not the cells but the fluid around them that deteriorates and causes aging and death. By renewing the fluid at regular intervals he proved living cells could theoretically be kept alive forever. Unlike bulk water, the <u>cellular fluid,</u> which Dr. Carrell refers to, <u>is composed of crystals.</u>

For centuries Native American Indians have known that semi-precious gemstones possess healing qualities. Katrina Raphaell, *Crystal Enlightenment* and Barbara Brennan, *Hands of Light*, have raised healing with gemstones to new heights. Ja'neel Nagy first introduced me to crystals when I took a crystal-healing course from her twelve years ago.

Crystals work by pulsating, amplifying and intermingling their electromagnetic energy with that of corresponding organs and chakras. Green stones placed on the heart chakra heal heavy emotions and balances out grief and pain. They evoke forgiveness and stimulate love of self and universal love. There are many wonderful green stones that promote healing:

135

APATITE – promotes strength through spiritual oneness and love

ADVENTURINE – brings in the higher green energy ray of forgiveness

BLOODSTONE – brings courage, longevity and wealth

DIOPTASE – promotes strength of mind and will power

EMERALD – helps one go with the flow of life

FLOURITE – balances mind and spirit and body and emotions

GREEN ONYX – centers and aligns the body with higher powers

JADE – powerful emotional balance that dispels negativity

JASPER – creates a vibration of awareness

LARIMAR – healing work at the soul level

MALACHITE – enhances and amplifies

MOLDAVITE – brings about resolution

MOSS AGATE – imparts strength and courage

VARISCITE – opens up channel between physical and spiritual plane

TOURMALINE – strong protective influence

LOVE

What feeds the heart is love. It is truly at the center of all healing. Emmet Fox, author of *The Golden Gate*, says that "it makes no difference how hopeless the outlook, how muddled the tangle, how great the mistake, a sufficient realization of love will dissolve it all. And according to Dr. Robert Anthony Kreucher, author of *Harmonious Healing*, challenges of the heart chakra revolve around the tendency towards a fearful repression of love, which is a manifestation of self-centeredness. The lesson of the heart chakra is to integrate personal love with universal love and perceive the oneness of life. This acknowledges that all is in divine order.

"Unconditional love comes from the idea of serving, giving, bestowing, sharing and co-operating. It creates joy and confidence and is living in accordance with Divine Law. We can choose to live, labor and love in our own time knowing that what comes to us as seed may go to the next generation as blossom and that which comes as blossom may go forth as fruit."

NOW THIS IS TRULY THE SEED ATOM OF THE HEART

BLOSSOMING INTO THE LOVE CHILD OF TOMORROW.

"HEALING IS LOVE'S FINAL DESTINATION

WITHOUT LOVE THERE IS NO HEALING

WITH LOVE HEALING IS INEVITABLE."

(Scott and Shannon Peck)

BIBLIOGRAPHY

For More Information on Vibrational Therapy

Harmonious Healing: A Journey in Vibrational Medicine and Essene Living, Dr. Robert Anthony Kreucher, Ann Arbor, Michigan, Colossos Printing, 1998, (1-800-284-0776), $17.00.

Harmony of Science and Nature: Ways of Staying Healthy in a Modern World, John and Lucie Davidson, Cambridge, England, St. Edmundsbury Press ltd, 1991.

Vibrational Medicine for the 21st Century: The Complete Guide to Energy Healing and Spiritual Transformation, Dr. Richard Gerber, M.D., New York, N.Y., Harper-Collins Publishers, Inc., 2000.

SCENT

The Aromatherapy Handbook: The Secret Healing Power of Essential Oils, Daniele Ryman, London, England, Century Publishing, 1984.

The Art of Aromatherapy, Robert Tisserand, London, England, Tisserand Aromatherapy, 1996.

Anoint Yourself with Oil – For Radiant Health, David Richard, Bloomingdale, Illinois, Vital Health Publishing 1997.

FEELING

How to Remember the Bach Flower Remedies, Joyce Petrak, DCH, Warren, Michigan, Curry Peterson Press, 1992.

The Twelve Healers of the Zodiac – The Astrology Handbook of the Bach Flower Remedies, Peter Damian, York Beach, Maine, Samuel Weiser, Inc. 1986.

MAGNETISM

Know you Magnetic Field, William E. Gray, Manuscript by the mysterious Mr. A. in Ruth Montgomery's books.

Magnetism – and Its Effects on The Living System, Albert Roy Davis and Walter C. Rawls Jr., Kansas City, Missouri, Acres U.S.A., 1974.

The Ultimate Healing System, Donald Lepore, N.D., Jersey City, New Jersey, Woodland Publishing, Inc., 1985.

ELECTRICAL CURRENT

The Cancer Cure, Barry Lynes, Canada, Marcus Books, 1987.

Purchasing the Rife Machine – John Wright Laboratories www.jwlabs.com, Approximate cost - $700.00.

A Search for the Truth & Born to Heal - Ruth Montgomery, New York, N.Y., Fawcett Crest Books, 1966, 1973.

Any inquiries concerning Mr. A can be addressed to Life Energies Research Foundation, Suite 406, 3808 Riverside Drive, Burbank, California 91505.

OSCILLATING FREQUENCY

The Chi Machine – for more information go to www.hteusa.com or call Hsin Ten Enterprises USA, Inc. at 1-800-547-1510. To Purchase a Chi Machine my sponsor ID# is A151701. You can sign up to be a distributor, sponsor others or just purchase products.

Billye Graham

SOUND

BioAcoustics – Sharry Edwards,
www.soundhealthinc.com, www.shri.html-reports,
www.thedaviscenter.com.

LIGHT – COLOR THERAPY

Color Preference Analysis – Potentials Unlimited, Inc., Dept. SP, P.O. Box 891, Grand Rapids, Michigan 49518.

Color Me A Season Educational Color Corp. 1651 Thornwood Drive, Concord, California, 94521 (415 676-9184).

Color Therapy Eyewear, Terri Perrigoue-Messer, Diamond Springs, California.

HEART

The Hearts Code, **Paul Pearsall, Ph.D., New York, N.Y., Broadway Books, 1998.**

CRYSTAL THERAPY

Crystal Enlightenment, Katrina Raphael, Santa Fe, New Mexico, Aurora Press, 1985.

Hands of Light, Barbara Brennan, New York, N.Y. Bantam Books, 1987.

Love is in the Earth, Melody, Wheat Ridge, Colorado, Earth-Love Publishing House, 1995.

Voices of Our Ancestors – Cherokee Teachings From The Wisdom Fire, Dhyani Ywahoo, Boston, Massachusetts, Shambhala Publications, Inc., 1987.

LOVE

Power through Constructive Thinking -The Golden Gate, The Emmet Fox Treasury, New York, N.Y., Harper and Row, 1979.

"Healing is Love's Final Destination," Scott and Shannon Peck, Phenomenews, December 1999, page 65.

CHAPTER NINE

A DIALOGUE OF TESTIMONIALS

TESTIMONIALS

What follows are a number of miraculous testimonials about the healing properties of wheat grass. Even though a myriad of illnesses are discussed wheat grass has helped no matter the cause or circumstances. One of the myths of disease is that there are many kinds.

There is one disease - disharmony and one cure - balance.

I would also like to mention that many of the people in these testimonials opted for allopathic procedures along with alternative measures like wheat grass. It is my strong belief that wheat grass better prepares the human body for invasive procedures and provides strength and endurance afterwards.

FACE IT WITH A SMILE

I don't think there is anything more frightening to a parent than receiving a phone call informing them that their child has been in an accident and is hurt. I received such a phone call on January 20, 2000 at 9:15 p.m. I had just returned from the auto show, at Cobo Hall in Detroit, and rushed into the house to pick up the ringing phone. "Mrs. Graham this is Tom. David is in the hospital. He's been in a car accident and I've been trying to reach you for hours."

You don't know what to think when they won't even let you see your child. He was covered with so much blood they thought he had been shot and cut his clothes off. In reality he had been at the wrong place at the wrong time trying to do a noble deed for a female friend in distress and had the side of a car door window kicked into his face lacerating it and cutting an artery too close to his eye to even mention.

I don't know which one hurt me the most, the wounded look on his face or the 25 stitches down the side of it. The very first thing I did upon arriving home was to take off the bandages and bath the wound in liquid wheat grass. We were to return to the hospital in five days and I wanted to give him the best chance possible for minimal scarring and maximum healing.

When we returned to the hospital the attending nurse was astounded. "What did you do to this wound? I've never seen a wound heal like this before. It is not tight and there is no encrustation. The skin is nearly knitted back together and the swelling has gone down considerably." Of course I told her about wheat grass and it's incredible healing properties on skin lacerations and wounds.

It's been three years now and my son still does not want to consider plastic surgery. There are still razor thin marks on the side of his face but when asked about getting the surgery he replies: "sometimes you have to face things with a smile and wear your war wounds well."

MANAGING A STINK

My husband, Al was having some problems with constipation and I suggested that he take seven wheat grass tablets before going to work. When I got home that evening I asked him about the results. "Oh boy did they work! Why didn't you tell me this stuff was going to clean me out! I was supposed to be in management meetings all day long and all I met and consulted with was every stall in every bathroom in the building. Outside of being embarrassed about excusing himself all day, he did admit that he felt better and swore that he had lost ten pounds in the process.

LEND ME YOUR EAR

I will never forget the day my son returned home from the mall with by husband in tow, both sporting a diamond-studded earring in the left ear. Al was too ashamed to raise his head for well over an hour so that I could get the full effect of what had been done.

David was still young and in high school, but soon found that most jobs frowned on men with earrings. Finally he took a job at the airport assisting physically and mentally challenged passengers and the earring had to go. My worst fears were realized when he began to form a keloid behind his ear. The rigors of youth had made him too undisciplined to follow alternative health measures so he finally decided to have it surgically removed. I instructed him that he must bath the ear in liquid wheat grass morning, noon and night if he didn't want the keloid to return.

Dr. Jackson wanted him to come for quarterly check-ups for about a year. But just shy of four months she felt confident that the keloid was not re-growing and required no further visits. It truly is nice when our children finally lend us their ears and listen to our advice. Most honoring is when they follow through and successfully resolve a health challenge.

THE JAMAICAN CONNECTION

After trying wheat grass for about a week my Jamaican colleague Glenn exclaimed: "mon, you'd better give me two more bottles of this stuff. I tell you I can last twice as long with the ladies! I'm going to send you all my countrymen from Jamaica who work here. I've told them this stuff is better than Viagra and I just love the fact that it is an all natural food! As a matter of fact give me another bottle to send to my friend in Chicago! Wow girl, thank you for introducing me to wheat grass!"

FREE YOUR MIND THE REST WILL FOLLOW

My friend Laura is a big girl, 5' 11" tall and some wide. She was a meat and potatoes girl who didn't want to even entertain the idea of eating something green. She heard about an operation where they staple your stomach and remove a part of your intestines. For two long years all I heard about was "when I have this surgery I'm going to lose all this weight."

Well as God would have it, Laura was told time and time again that her health challenges that included diabetes, overweight and a medium sized ovarian tumor, would not allow for an operation of this kind. Finally Laura resigned herself to the fact that she was going to have to lose some weight before she could qualify for this surgery.

She began to read more about health and settled on Coral Calcium as her miracle pill. Rather than dissuade her I simply suggested that she take wheat grass along with it. After several months of carefully watching what she ate and drank (seeds, nuts, fruit, fish, chicken, raw green salads) Laura was shocked when she found out that she had lost a whopping 40 pounds. All that hard work of changing diet and habit had paid off. I was delighted to hear her say that after gaining so much knowledge

about health that this procedure didn't seem very healthy or appealing to her anymore.

REACH OUT AND TOUCH SOMEONE

There isn't a person at Northwest Airlines who hasn't heard me extol the wonders of wheat grass. You never know when the seed you have planted in people's minds will germinate. Yet I was completely surprised when our secretary Alexis asked for two bottles of wheat grass tablets - one for herself and one for her mother.

A couple of weeks later Alexis' mother dropped by my house and purchased several more bottles of wheat grass – one for her son and one for her friend Mrs. Sanders who ironically lived right down the street from me.

THE GOLDEN GIRLS

Soon Mrs. Sanders began buying several bottles of wheat grass a week. It wasn't very long before people began to comment on how beautiful her skin looked. Her face just radiated this golden glow of health and she started to lose weight even though that was not her goal. She was so elated with her energy high that she started talking to her friends about it on the way to work. In short order I had nine new customers including the bus driver who drove them to work. He had listened and looked long enough and wanted to try wheat grass for himself.

I tried to tell Mrs. Sanders about the other benefits of wheat grass but she was only interested in how great it made her feel. She was not interested in giving up meat, cigarette smoking or alcohol. She had had several heart attacks before she started taking wheat grass and nine months later she had another mild one. Whether it was a healing crisis or bad habits that triggered it we will never know. But the situation now had her attention.

Billye Graham

THE LOST SHEEP

One day Mrs. Sanders decided to buy my wheat grass book. I was really surprised when she showed up again, the next day with a friend in tow. His name is Joe. She was excited and told me that Joe had something he wanted to tell me. "I have been an alcoholic for longer that I care to remember. But I can remember a time when health was important to me. I was so intrigued by what you had to say about wheat grass that I wanted to try those pills right then and there. I stayed up all night and read your book three times. At seven o'clock I eagerly took seven tablets. By noon I usually would be on my third or fourth drink of the day. But today, I want you to know, it is 4:00 o'clock in the afternoon and I haven't even wanted a drink. I want to thank you for sharing your knowledge of wheat grass with me. If you ever need my help in growing it just let me know." Just as a shepherd must leave his flock to find the sheep that go astray, wheat grass has redeemed a lost soul.

SLEEPING BEAUTY

I work for Northwest Airlines and Sam is one of the fuelers working with me. Sam had sleep apnea so bad that he would fall asleep in mid sentence while conversing with you. One day at work I awakened Sam from one of his stupors and offered him seven wheat grass tablets and a three-day supply to keep him going.

Sam returned at the end of the week with a glowing report. "I've been on this breathing machine at night for about a week. They tell me that out of eight hours I am only breathing for about five. I don't like this mask over my nose so I took those wheat grass tablets and guess what? They told me my breathing had improved to the point where I don't need to use this machine at night any more. And guess what else? I need some more of that wheat grass!"

FUELING THE FUELERS

As a result of Sam's very visible and dramatic results from wheat grass I soon found myself selling wheat grass to nearly all of the fuelers. Adrian became my number one customer. He worked sixteen hours a day for months on end from the energy wheat grass supplied. But he was more impressed with how "cut and buff his body was becoming," as he also worked out. Delon would tease me by asking me to sell him another "dime bag" of wheat grass, although I was only selling it for $8.00 dollars a bottle. Jimmy, a fueling supervisor, was dragging from exhaustion. After just one day of taking wheat grass he said it just picked him right up off the floor. Pizz took wheat grass faithfully for about a year. This was the first time he could remember going through the whole winter without coming down with a cold.

Billye Graham

THE AFRICAN CONNECTION

My friend Milton returned from his first trip to Africa with an organism he picked up that was affecting his nervous system. I told him of my newfound health habits; living foods and wheat grass. I also pointed him in the direction of Thelma Curtis. She is the Director of the Healing Support Network and prepares macrobiotic and living food meals in her home. Milton became a regular dinner guest and at the end of nine months was fit as a fiddle. He never turns down a shot of wheat grass and travels the world over now without getting sick.

Carol, another colleague of mind, came back from Africa with malaria. She spent three days at my house while I administered wheat grass and suggested she try urine therapy. Since this health challenge she has made innumerable trips across the waters to Europe and Africa and not gotten sick.

THE GLOBETROTTER

Linell has always been one of my favorite "young colleagues." She has a beautiful smile with pearly white teeth that compliments her deep chocolate complexion. She always exudes a refreshing up-beat outlook on life colored by intelligence and genuine friendliness. It pained me greatly to hear the deep hurt in her voice when she recounted to me a most disturbing story. She had just returned from Europe and found out that she had meningitis. Meningitis is an acute infection of the membranes of the brain and considered highly contagious. Without complications recovery from meningitis generally takes about three weeks.

Linell had been released to return to work only to be met by hostile co-workers who had once been friends of long standing. She was asked by management to leave the premises even though she had a doctor's notice clearing her of contagious status. Devastated by this reception she had phoned me in hopes of advice and solace. My first question was where had she been and what had she been eating since meningitis is caused by poor nutrition in combination with any number of bacteria and viruses. Over the last six months she had partied in Aruba (the Caribbean) shopped till she dropped in Beijing (the Orient) and "Jet Set" to London and Paris (Europe). Well no wonder she was

ill. As a travel veteran I knew she had over done it. The body needs time to adjust and re-adjust to different water, climates, food and surroundings, not to mention that rest is essential to globetrotting!

When I went to Linell's house that night she appeared pale, ashen, gaunt and weak. I brought her liquid wheat grass and wheat grass tablets along with oil of oregano and other immune building herbs, minerals and vitamins. Inside of two weeks her own mother commented on how much better she looked and Linell concurred by telling all who would listen about how much better she actually felt. I extracted a promise from her that she would be still for at least a year. I also made her promise that when she resumed traveling she would faithfully take wheat grass tablets to give her stamina and protection.

HIGH ENERGY

Curlee really likes airplanes and aerodynamics. He works with me at Northwest Airlines, has his own private pilot's license and is currently pursuing a teaching degree in aviation. All this spells long hours of working, studying, flying and going to school. Curlee was perpetually tired and exhibited a lot of nervous energy. Of course I told him about wheat grass tablets and he tried them. He became more energized stating that four to five hours of sleep now left him feeling rested. Also his countenance changed to a somewhat calmer tempo.

Billye Graham

THE SHINING

William is a retired autoworker and runs a shoeshine stand at the airport. I had noticed for several weeks that he had been missing from work and inquired as to his health. Sure enough he had had a stroke. When he finally returned to work his speech was slurred and a slight down turn of the lower lip at the corner was noticeable. I promptly told him about wheat grass and he promptly bought some from me on the spot. This was some years ago and his health has improved tremendously. No more slurred speech or drooping mouth. Instead the shining signatures of wheat grass are present - glowing skin and visible weight loss. Every time I see him he still thanks me for his improved health. And every time I thank him for having the good sense to try wheat grass and continuing to take it.

BLOOD SPORT

When my son David was twelve years old I enrolled him in a karate class. During the customary interview with the karate instructor the subject of health and sports injuries came up. He had a leg amputated and the prosthesis he wore had recently been covered with a skin graft at the knee. He had tried everything but the graft continued to bleed. I offered him my wheat grass pulp as a poultice and instructed him to wrap his knee at night with an ace bandage.

Several weeks later I was startled when the instructor rang my bell bright and early on a Sunday morning. He had come to thank me. The bleeding had stopped. He was simply grateful that wheat grass had done this marvelous deed.

THE EYES HAVE IT

Glaucoma

My uncle Chuck smokes like a chimneystack, drinks like a fish, cusses like a sailor and fusses like a woman. Well it all caught up with him in his "golden years" manifesting in several semi-paralyzing strokes. He now walks with a walker, has slurred speech and not a lot of range of motion in his arms.

The wake up call he finally understood was when the hospital wanted to remove his left eye due to glaucoma (built up pressure in the eye due to lack of proper fluid drainage). Nutrition has been identified as all-important in the cure and prevention of this disease.

My aunt Catheryne called upon us all to send him money to defray the cost of eye drops $108.00 monthly that was not covered by Medicaid. I sent money but I also took a chance and sent my uncle two bottles of wheat grass tablets, as he seemed intent upon not having this surgery.

"Is it possible that this stuff can really work that fast? I've only been taking it for three days and I really felt better the first day. Now I'm up cooking fish and eating it too. I haven't cooked in years and I have the energy, from God knows where, to stand on my feet for several hours at a time." My uncle did well for about six months until the holidays rolled around. Unfortunately his newfound enthusiasm didn't outlast his life long love affair with bad habits. He is now in a nursing home but he still has both of his eyes.

Cataracts

Phyllis was a slow starter on wheat grass. She simply could not determine that she was feeling any better by taking it. I told her to stick with the program for at least a month and see if she could tell any difference by then. About six weeks later she told me she just felt better, nothing specific just better. When Phyllis went for her most recent eye exam she had been taking wheat grass for a little over a year.

"You know I am developing cataracts (a disease of the eye lens that impairs and destroys vision) and my optometrist felt that somewhere down the road I would have to have them removed. But my most recent eye exam revealed no further development and the cataracts were actually regressing. Now I haven't done anything different this past year except take wheat grass. Do you think this stuff is actually reversing this condition?"

I replied, that wheat grass has wrought many a miracle and I had no doubt it was doing the same for her.

Glasses

I hadn't had an eye exam for nearly three years. I don't like wearing glasses because I know you develop a dependency on them. Although I do a number of things to strengthen my eyes (wash them out with urine and The Master's Miracle Neutralizer, eat plenty of carrots, do eye exercises and of course take wheat grass) I do rely on glasses for reading.

Although I was dreading the verdict that I needed bifocals, I had put this off long enough. To my surprise and delight the eye exam revealed very little change over the past three years. I was even given the choice of sticking with regular glasses or the bifocals. There was no contest. I chose the reading glasses and knew that wheat grass had played an integral part in preserving my vision.

ISSUES

It is my solemn belief that behind every health challenge are life issues that people are not coping with very well. My aunt Vernice had noticed a lump in her breast about six months before she found the courage to go and have it tested. One could only wonder why she had let so much time lapse, especially given the fact that she was a registered nurse for fifty years.

I had a nice long talk with my aunt and finally understood the issues that had brought her to this health challenge. Her husband had died several years earlier and had left no provisions for her financially. She had her youngest son living with her who was between jobs and my Uncle Chuck living downstairs who was a semi-invalid. At age seventy six she was paying all the bills on a two family flat, cooking for three people and making a gallant effort to keep up her relationships with her other five children, their children and spouses. I calmly asked her how she felt they all would get along without her should she perish from this serious health challenge. I also told her that at this point the only person she needed to be concerned about was herself.

She had been diagnosed with breast cancer and cancer of the esophagus. She had sounded weak over the phone and more than a little despondent. I had sent two bottles of wheat grass tablets to her several weeks before my sister and I arrived for a visit. She didn't sound very much like she was interested in taking them. So I was totally taken aback when she came floating down the stairs in a bright floral caftan, smiling and looking like a radiant angel. "Well, she said, I thought about what you said and decided to try the tablets you sent me. After a few days I began to feel better, my appetite returned and I just got a burst of energy. You saw me come down the stairs to greet you! I don't seem to be in pain and I just feel so much better."

My aunt opted for chemotherapy. The treatments took her appetite away and she was unable to swallow so the wheat grass pills became null and void. Three months later my aunt Vernice passed away. Silently I thanked her for her bravery. She had tried something new that flew in the face of all that she had been taught and held dear.

WINNING

It was only one month after we had visited my aunt Vernice that my sister Sherry hit us with a double whammy – she too had breast cancer. Armed with a suitcase of alternative therapies I began to outline to my sister what she would need to do to turn the tide of this health challenge. She had known for four years that she had breast cancer and it had spread to her lymph system.

She started on wheat grass and essiac's tea immediately and decided to come to the Creative Health Institute for therapeutic support. After six weeks she consulted both an allopathic doctor and a holistic practitioner who both confirmed to her that the cancer was in remission. My sister elected to have a mastectomy anyway and underwent chemotherapy afterwards for six months. I urged her to continue taking wheat grass and barley green along with these treatments, which she did. On New Year's Day she called with the good news that she was cancer free and she has remained so for the past four years.

SUGARLESS

My father had been a diabetic for seventeen years and became curious about wheat grass as a result of the successful resolution of my health challenge. He still cooked in aluminum pots (which everyone knows causes Alzheimer's disease) and ate everything boiled, fried, stewed, canned and dead. I supplied him with two bottles of wheat grass and waited to hear from him.

About two weeks later he called me and was eager to relay what had happened at his monthly check-up meeting with the doctor.

"Mr. Suttles I don't know what you've done, but your sugar is normal and you need to stop taking your insulin." For whatever reasons my father decided to stop taking the wheat grass tablets instead. Changes on a physical plane necessarily need to be accompanied by changes on the mental and spiritual plane if the change is to withstand the test of time. My father passed on some years later from a heart attack.

ORGAN GRINDER

Kidneys are organs that distill liquids from the bowel and redistribute nutrients into the blood stream. Any excess is passed out of the body through the bladder as urine. You can exist with one kidney but two down is a lose-lose situation.

Ruby, a family friend, came by my house one day and asked if I thought wheat grass might help her with a circulation problem. Her legs were so swollen and tight that they felt like sand paper to the touch. She was diabetic, had glaucoma and was now faced with the fact that her kidneys were not filtering or moving toxins out of her body.

I offered her fresh wheat grass juice but the most I could get her to try was the wheat grass tablets. About a month later she was told that she was in complete renal failure and dialysis was necessary three times a week. After six months of dialysis she confided in me that she was still urinating on her own. Eventually with the onslaught of dialysis and the discontinuance of the tablets her bodily functions did become completely dependent on the machine. It is said that dialysis shaves off fifteen years of your life. Ruby was sixty-three when she made her transition. She had survived dialysis for five years.

LIFE IN THE FAST LANE

Dennis had aids. He was a tall light skinned brother with all the two snaps and a twist lingo of his lifestyle. I met him at the Creative Health Institute about ten years ago and his praise for wheat grass and lambs quarters went something like this: "I get sassy when I take this stuff! I've got pep in my step, a tiger in my tank and I am too hot to trot!! It's better than those hormone pills I've been takin."

All that energy is gone now. Dennis liked his lifestyle better than his life. About a year later he traded one for the other and made his peace. I think of Dennis when I hear about celebrities with aids. And I often wonder with all of their wealth and resources, why the rich and famous have yet to discover wheat grass.

Billye Graham

STREET SMARTS

The most profound story I ever read about wheat grass and it's ability to affect a cure was written by Dr. Morton Walker. He tape recorded a health history of Bennie Slopp who had been treated by Howard Besoza, M.D., an holistic physician practicing in New York City.

"For thirty-six of his fifty-four years, Bennie Slopp has lived the lousiest of lifestyles on the streets of congested cities around the United States. He is a long time drinker consuming cheap wine or whiskey and a smoker, smoking up to four packs of unfiltered camels a day. He is skinny as a rail and eats from the garbage cans of fast food restaurants. Occasionally he will buy packaged convenience food. Bennie is dirty nearly all of the time. He never changes clothes and takes a shower at the Turkish baths or the YMCA maybe once in two weeks when be can afford it."

Bennie Slopp consulted Dr. Besoza in 1997 and was diagnosed with an inoperable malignant tumor obliterating both his hard and soft palates. This is a deadly cancer but Bennie didn't die; instead he experienced a complete cancer remission. By some means he found out about sweet wheat, a freeze-dried form of wheat grass.

Along with his use of allopathic medicine consisting of radiation treatments twice a day Bennie rinsed his mouth with organic wheat grass powder dissolved in lukewarm water. He gargled and swirled the wheat grass around his oral cavity for perhaps sixty seconds, then swallowed the green liquid. In one months time, and after twenty-eight x-ray treatments, not only did Bennie Slopp undergo cancer remission but also reduced the size of the original tumor until it disappeared altogether. He experienced none of the adverse side effects expected from radiation therapy. And it was also determined that the type of cancer he had would not have responded that quickly to radiation therapy alone.

Somehow the word has gotten out on the streets about wheat grass but not in loftier circles. Street people tell me that inside of ten days of using wheat grass they are able to pass a urine test with no drug deposits registering in their system.

GROWTH REDUCTION

My conversations with my aunt Catheryne were marathon sessions and invariably we talked about health. I finally convinced her to try wheat grass as she often spoke about how tired she was since she entered her "golden years." After several weeks she called to tell me "those wheat grass tablets did the trick girl! I'm even riding my stationary bike again."

It was a year later, however that she mentioned to me something of a more serious nature. "You know last year this time I had a mammogram done and they found a lump. I did not opt for a biopsy but I faithfully took those wheat grass tablets you told me about. I was pleased as punch this year when they found no trace of that lump."

Billye Graham

A DOG'S BARK AND A CAT'S MEOW

Every pet owner knows that cats and dogs endorse grass since that is what they eat when they are sick. We applaud their instincts as bloodhounds, their hearing alacrity and their instinctual likes and dislikes of people. But somehow we have overlooked their fundamental understanding of healing and wellness. Instead of offering them grass when they are sick we take them to a veterinarian.

JJ, my dog's babysitter, is a veterinarian technician. She owns eight Pugs of her own and her house is a virtual zoo with all the babysitting she does. One of her older dogs was not growing old gracefully and had repeat bowel and bladder problems. The wheat grass tablets I gave her helped she said.

I even suggested wheat grass to my sales lady at The House of Denmark Furniture Store. Her dog had a bowel obstruction. She went out and bought a whole tray of fresh wheat grass from a local health food store. She was pleased to tell me at our next meeting that the dog was doing just fine, thanks to me and wheat grass.

Kim, a co-worker, bought wheat grass for her dog. He had a problem with constipation. He be-

197

Billye Graham

came so regular and frequent that she can only give him wheat grass now on her days off. She was so impressed that she began taking them herself and got her uncle started too.

My dog Zeus developed a limp. She's a large boned German Shepard mixed with Terrier. I understand that as large dogs age their limbs can become arthritic. Several days of applying liquid wheat grass to her limbs and joints made everything right. That was several years ago and she has shown no more signs of arthritis.

SEIZE THE MOMENT

Nancy has always been a good friend of mine, and one of my favorite co-workers at Northwest Airlines. Fourteen years ago she gave birth to Andrew. He was born with cerebral palsy. This health challenge affects the control of voluntary muscular movements. It can produce weakness, paralysis, lack of coordination, tremors, and rigidity or spasticity. Epilepsy is often associated with cerebral palsy. Epilepsy is characterized by abnormal brain wave patterns that result in seizures. Nutrition is important to those who suffer from epilepsy especially choline (found in wheat grass). It is a natural anti-convulsant. Cerebral palsy is also linked to allergies associated with food, water and air.

At the age of eleven Andrew developed epilepsy and by age fourteen was having up to forty seizures a day. The lack of normal movement resulted in a loss of muscle tone and a sluggish immune system. His body simply lacked the ability to remove toxicity. I suggested to Nancy that she try wheat grass therapy. Nancy reported that the first dose of liquid wheat grass cut the seizures in half, down from forty a day to twenty. While on vacation the next week she agreed to administer seven wheat grass tablets daily to Andrew.

It was several weeks later that we actually had an opportunity to talk again. "Well Billye this stuff really cleaned him out. As a matter of fact I found myself washing and changing his clothes two to three times a day. I even had to pull him out of school for three days! Is this normal or is this some sort of side effect she queried?" I assured her it was quite normal and probably from the sounds of things very much needed.

When I asked Nancy about the seizures, a frozen look of surprise came over her face. "Billye, I was so taken aback with the clean up process that I completely forgot about the seizures. Now that you mention it he hasn't had a single one in three weeks. My God, do you really think it's the wheat grass.?! Yes, I said along with the grace of God. It has been almost nine months and Andrew is still free of seizures.

EMPOWERMENT

One Sunday afternoon, my friend and mentor, Hiawatha came from Lansing and invited me to a testimonial banquet. A couple that had recently completed her living foods lifestyle program gave it. She was on the panel of people they wished to honor. "Now I don't have to speak on wheat grass," I asked? "Oh no, Hiawatha assured me, you can just sit in the audience this time."

Mrs. Charles was the moderator and I was very impressed with her presentation on wheat grass. She seemed very knowledgeable. As usual, Hiawatha volunteered me to make a few comments to add to her presentation since I had written a book on the subject. I stepped up to the podium and to my surprise there lay an open copy of my book that Mrs. Charles had been reading from and referring to.

I smiled and told the audience that I was very impressed with the moderator's knowledge of wheat grass and was pleasantly surprised that she was using my book as a reference guide. "She is really smarter than me," I said. She brought my book here and I didn't even bring any copies!

A GREEN THUMB

To my further delight, Mr. Charles gave another glorious testimonial. He had been diagnosed with cancer of the esophagus a year to the date of this testimonial living foods banquet. He worked in a dry cleaner business and was exposed to chemicals on a daily basis. Mr. Charles was given only months to live and the couple frantically began to seek out alternatives to allopathic medicine. They located an iridologist who felt the condition Mr. Charles had was treatable. He was the one who directed them to contact Hiawatha and she in turn introduced them to wheat grass therapy.

Mr. Charles followed me to the podium and proudly announced that he had been cancer free for one year. This was a celebration of that accomplishment and he had many people to thank for it. "I followed the simple instructions in Mrs. Graham's book, about how to grow wheat grass and am now growing up to twelve trays a week." There before us were his trays of "green gold" and the line was wrapped around the corner for samples. I was extremely moved, pleased, proud and honored to witness this moment in time.

Billye Graham

REPEAT PERFORMANCE

Iyanla Vanzant, the popular author of many inspirational books, talks about her humble beginnings. *Acts of Faith*, her first major book was done in soft cover because the publishers were not sure of it's market value. Well it went on to become so popular that people began to write for another copy. Their first ones had become torn and worn out through use. They also urged her to consider a hard cover edition this time and the rest is history.

Well, I haven't reached such lofty heights as this but it was heart warming to receive the following post card and follow up note from Zema. I was thrilled that something I had created was valued enough that someone else would not want to be without it.

Billye Graham

I DON'T BELIEVE IN MIRACLES

I COUNT ON THEM

Billye Graham

Well, I haven't reached such lofty heights as this but it was heart warming to receive the following post card and follow up note from Zema. I was thrilled that something I had created was valued enough that someone else would not want to be without it.

Note: I purchased a copy of Hiawatha's Cookbook, and I saw where you collaborated in its production. I want to commend you all on a superb job!!!

Aug. 22, 2002

Hello Billye;
I tried calling you about a week ago but I was not able to get through. What I want is a copy of your mailing on Wheat Grass and all of its benefits. I bought a copy from you in 1998 or 1999 at Ebenezar Church when you and Hiawatha did a workshop there for Barbara Calloway. I have misplaced my copy. I have forgotten the price. So if you have more copies, please send me a copy along with the price + mailing cost. I'll remit same by return mail. Thanks — ZEMA

Hello Billye:

Thanks for the publication. Wow! It is so great! I wasn't expecting such a fantastic compilation of information and wheat-grass know how.

My misplacing the original copy of your material was a blessing in disguise, believe me; for I would have never known about this wonderful publication. Again, I thank you.

Enclosed is a check to cover the cost plus shipping. ($12.50)

Zema

About the Author

Mrs. Billye J. Graham

Lecturer
Alternative Health Consultant
Wheat Grass Specialist

With a name like "Billye Graham" you are bound to preach about something! And preach she does, never missing an opportunity to talk about health as well as sing the praises of wheat grass.

Billye has been a health minister for 15 years and a health practitioner for 25 years. Allopathic medicine failed to answer her questions or provide solutions to some very serious health challenges. Holistic health did. She has enlightened many people by sharing her triumph over dis-ease through the discovery and use of wheat grass therapy.

She practices the living foods lifestyle, operates A New Start Health and Wellness Center and makes wheat grass the cornerstone of all her teachings and wellness programs.

CONTACT:
E-Mail: bgraham137@earthlink.net

LaVergne, TN USA
10 December 2010
208347LV00003B/63/A